A
BELIEVER'S
GUIDE TO
SPIRITUAL
FITNESS

Light for Your Path

The Light for Your Path Series is for women who desire to know, love, and serve God better. Each book is designed to nurture new believers while challenging women who are ready for deeper study. Studies in the series examine *books* of the Bible, on the one hand (look for subtitles beginning with *Light from*), and important *topics* in Christian faith and life, on the other (look for subtitles beginning with *Focus on*). The series blends careful instruction with active reader participation in a variety of study exercises, always encouraging women to live in the light of biblical truth in practical ways.

Two foundational studies explain why and how to study the Bible as the one perfect light source for your Christian walk:

A Book Like No Other: What's So Special About the Bible
Turning On the Light: Discovering the Riches of God's Word

Also available:

The Light for Your Path Series Leader's Guide
God with Us: Light from the Gospels
Before the Throne of God: Focus on Prayer
His Witnesses to the World: Light from Acts

A
BELIEVER'S
GUIDE TO
SPIRITUAL
FITNESS

Focus on His Strength

Carol J. Ruvolo

P&R
P U B L I S H I N G
P.O.BOX 817 • PHILLIPSBURG • NEW JERSEY 08865-0817

Unless otherwise indicated, Scripture quotations are from the New American Standard Bible. Copyright by the Lockman Foundation 1960, 1962, 1963, 1968, 1971, 1973, 1975, 1977. Italics indicate emphasis added.

Printed in the United States of America

Composition by Colophon Typesetting
Cover design by Now You See it!

Library of Congress Cataloging-in-Publication Data

Ruvolo, Carol J., 1946–
    A believer's guide to spiritual fitness : focus on His strength / by Carol J. Ruvolo.
        p. cm. — (Light for your path)
    Includes bibliographical references.
    ISBN 0-87552-633-0 (pbk.)
        1. Christian women—Religious life. 2. Spiritual life— Reformed church.   I. Title.

BV4527 .R88 2000
248.8 43—dc21

00-038512

In loving memory of
Sarah Warren
(August 4, 1978—October 18, 1999),

and to her mother,
D. J. Warren,
whose spiritual strength
reflects God's power
perfected in weakness.

CONTENTS

PREFACE
Welcome to the Light for Your Path Series   ix

INTRODUCTION
The Friend   3

PART 1
The Mindset of Strength

LESSON 1
A Matter of Focus   11

PART 2
The Components of Strength

LESSON 2
The Life of Salvation   25

LESSON 3
The Good Bones of Knowledge   37

LESSON 4
The Muscles of Faith   49

LESSON 5
The Blood of Love   63

LESSON 6
The Skin of Fellowship   75

Contents

PART 3
The Spiritual Workout Routine

LESSON 7
Our Personal Spiritual Trainer   91

LESSON 8
The Good Diet of Scripture   103

LESSON 9
The Exercise of Obedience   117

LESSON 10
The Rejuvenating Rest of Prayer   131

PART 4
Three Devious Strength Stealers

LESSON 11
Laziness   143

LESSON 12
Neglect   157

LESSON 13
Disease and Injury   169

APPENDIX A
What Must I Do to Be Saved?   183

APPENDIX B
What Is the Reformed Faith?   189

RECOMMENDED READING   195

Welcome to the Light for Your Path Series

The Light for Your Path Series is designed to help women learn how to glorify and enjoy God by living out their transformation in Jesus Christ. Each book in the series reflects the author's commitment to the Bible as the infallible, inerrant, authoritative, and entirely sufficient Word of God, and her conviction that Reformed theology is the clearest and most accurate restatement of biblical truth.

The series begins with two foundational studies centering on the Bible itself. *A Book Like No Other: What's So Special About the Bible* presents (in six lessons) the unique character of God's revelation. *Turning On the Light: Discovering the Riches of God's Word* provides (in seven lessons) an effective approach to studying the Bible. Combining these two books in a thirteen-week course will prepare new and veteran students to gain the most from the Light for Your Path Series.

The remaining studies in the series fall into two categories. "Light" studies cover particular *books* of the Bible (or sections of books, or groups of books such as the Gospels). These studies guide you through portions of Scripture, enabling you to understand and apply the meaning of each passage. You will recognize them by their subtitles, beginning with the words *Light from*.

"Focus" studies spotlight important *topics* in the Christian faith and life, such as prayer, salvation, righteousness, and relationships, and seek to show what the whole Bible says about them. These studies also stress understanding and applying biblical truth in daily life. Their subtitles begin with the words *Focus on.* Studying a combination of biblical books and topics will shed much-needed scriptural light on your walk with God. Both types of Bible study should be included in a "balanced diet" for a growing Christian.

The *Leader's Guide* that accompanies this series contains a complete description of the purpose and format of these studies, along with helpful suggestions for leading women through them.

Bible study is a serious task that involves a significant investment of time and energy. Preparing yourself to study effectively will help you reap the greatest benefit from that investment. Study when you are well rested and alert. Try to find a time and place that is quiet, free of distractions, and conducive to concentration. Use a loose-leaf or spiral notebook to take notes on what you read and to do the exercises in this study. You may also want to develop a simple filing system so that you can refer to these notes in later studies.

Approach Bible study as you would any task that requires thought and effort to do well. Don't be surprised if it challenges you and stretches your thinking. Expect it to be difficult at times but extremely rewarding.

Always begin your study with prayer. Ask the Lord to reveal sin in your life that needs to be confessed and cleansed, to help you concentrate on His truths, and to illumine your mind with understanding of what He has written. End your study with a prayer for opportunities to apply what you have learned and wisdom to recognize those opportunities when they occur.

Each lesson in these studies is followed by three types of "Exercises": "Review," "Application," and "Digging Deeper." The *review* exercises will help you determine how well you understood the lesson material by giving you an opportunity to express the key points in your own words. The *application* exercises encourage you to put your understanding of the material to work in your daily life. And the *digging deeper* exercises challenge you to pursue further study in certain key areas.

You should be able to find the answers to the *review* questions in the lesson material itself, but please resist the temptation to copy words or phrases out of the lesson when you answer these questions. Work at putting these ideas into your own words. When you can do this, you know you have understood what you have read. It might help to ask yourself, "How would I explain this idea to someone else if I didn't have the book with me?"

If you don't have time to do all of the *application* exercises, pray over them and ask the Lord to show you which one(s) *He* wants you to work on. Because you will be applying the lessons to your daily life, these applications should take some time and thought. Answering one of them well will benefit you more than answering all of them superficially.

Answers to the application exercises should be very specific. Work at avoiding vague generalities. It might help to keep in mind that a specific application will answer the questions Who? What? When? Where? and How? A vague generality will not. You can make applications in the areas of your thinking, your attitudes, and your behavior. (See lesson 6 of *Turning On the Light* for more about application.)

Digging deeper exercises usually require a significant amount of time and effort to complete. They were designed to provide a challenge for mature Christians who are eager for more advanced study. However, new Christians should not automatically pass them by. The Holy Spirit may choose to use one of them to help you grow. Remember that *all Christians* grow by stretching beyond where they are right now. So if one or two of these exercises intrigue you, spend some time working on them. And do not hesitate to ask for help from your pastor, elders, or mature Christian friends.

As you work through this study, resist the temptation to compare yourself with other Christians in your group. The purpose of this study is to help you grow in your faith by learning and applying God's truth in your daily life—not to fill up a study book with brilliantly worded answers. If you learn and apply *one element* of God's truth in each lesson, you are consistently moving beyond where you were when you began.

Always remember that effective Bible study equips you *to glorify God and enjoy Him forever.* You glorify God when you live in such a way that those around you can look at you and see an accurate reflection of God's character and nature. You enjoy God when you are fully satisfied in His providential ordering of the circumstances in your life. When your life glorifies God and your joy is rooted in His providence, your impact on our fallen world will be tremendous.

An uncompromising life is characterized
by an unashamed boldness
that calls us to an uncommon standard.
Allow God to do with your life as He pleases,
that He might broaden your influence
and glorify Himself.
—John MacArthur

The Friend

The following story is fiction. Although certain elements of it were "lifted from life," the story does not, nor is it intended to, portray details of actual events.

— — —

Jodi smiled as she glanced at the name on the Caller ID and quickly answered the phone. "Hi there, old friend. What's new with you?"

"Jodi, I have something to tell you." Jodi's smile quickly dissolved in the realization that something was terribly wrong. There were tears in the voice of the woman she had rarely seen cry.

"Diana, what is it?" Jodi tightened her grip on the receiver and felt her stomach tighten as well. Had Diana's cancer jumped out of remission? Had Jeff's business taken yet another serious turn for the worse? *She could hear her friend draw a deep, quivering breath and then clear her throat. "Take your time, Diana. Just tell me what's happened."*

"Julie was on her way home for the weekend with Abbie. They were hit head-on by a drunk driver going the wrong way on the freeway." Jodi felt her knees buckle, and she reached for a chair.

Julie was Diana's eighteen-year-old daughter, a committed

Christian, away from home for the first time at the state university. She was rooming with Abbie, a quiet, sensitive girl who had grown up "moral and good" but completely devoid of spiritual training. Julie had patiently cultivated a close friendship with Abbie and had recently introduced her to Jesus Christ. Abbie seemed interested, but had not yet made a commitment. Julie had invited her new friend home for the Thanksgiving weekend, hoping the testimony of her close-knit Christian family might draw her closer to the Lord.

"Jodi," Diana's voice broke, and she paused a moment before going on. Jodi felt a cold wave of dread wash over her soul. "Julie was killed instantly. Abbie is critical. She was airlifted to Mercy, and the doctors are using words like 'guardedly hopeful.' The drunk driver walked away with minor injuries, but he's facing second-degree murder charges."

Jodi opened her mouth, desperately wanting to comfort this woman who had ministered to her so effectively for almost twenty-five years—long before either of them had married and had children. Now one of those children was dead. What could she possibly say? "Diana, I am so sorry," she finally gasped, wiping at the tears coursing down her own cheeks.

Diana's response caught Jodi completely off guard— although it shouldn't have because it was vintage Diana. "Oh, Jodi. God was so good to take Julie instead of Abbie. Julie was ready . . . and Abbie isn't." Diana's voice trailed off, and Jodi could sense her struggling. "And neither is that drunk driver. I know God's timing is perfect, and Julie's days on this earth were numbered before she was born. She was such a great blessing to us, and I'm grateful to God for lending her to us for eighteen years. But, Jodi—I'm going to miss her so much!" Diana sobbed audibly.

"We'll all miss her, dear friend. She was a blessing to everyone she encountered," Jodi said quietly, trying her best to wrap her words in a warm, secure hug Diana might sense without actually feeling.

Diana sighed deeply and blew her nose. When she finally spoke, Jodi knew she had tightened her grip on her unshakable faith. "She was, wasn't she! And would you believe she still is? I want to tell you how Jeff and I have already seen God use her death just as gloriously as He used her life."

Jodi marveled as she listened to her friend describe the many ways God had been pleased to work through Julie's death to glorify Himself and bring peace to His children in the midst of their sorrow. Diana and Jeff had quickly opened their home to Abbie's family and as a result had been able to forthrightly share with them the faith that fueled Julie's life and was now bringing comfort to her grieving loved ones.

Diana had reached out to the drunk driver's wife when she called to plead for forgiveness. The distraught woman's surprise at Diana's immediate assurance of complete forgiveness had opened another door for the gospel. Diana explained that she and Jeff could forgive because they had been forgiven. Jeff was now making plans to visit the man who had taken his daughter's life, and they were praying that his desperate situation might open his heart to receive God's gospel of grace.

"Diana," Jodi murmured when her friend finally paused. "I am amazed at your strength. I don't think I could respond as you have if it were Marty or Brenda. Maybe in six months or a year, but not within a few days. Where do you find that kind of strength at a time like this?"

"Jodi," Diana said softly. "I don't have any strength. I am the weakest of women. But God has strength enough for Himself, and for me, and for all of His children. And because He loves us so much, He's eager to share. All we need do is ask."

If you are like most Christians, you identify with Jodi more than you do with Diana. You marvel when you encounter such an exceptional example of spiritual strength. Your amazement may even have given way, in this case, to relieved incredulity as you thought to yourself, *Now wait a minute. It's only a story—pure fiction designed to convict and spur Christians to greater effort. Nobody really responds to disaster that way.*

If that's what you're thinking, I want to assure you that although the story is fictional, it is based on real responses to tragedy. It is a composite picture of the ways I have watched several strong Christian friends handle adversity. Interestingly, none of those people would have called themselves strong. In every case, they would have echoed Diana's affirmation that she was the weakest of women—and that spiritual strength comes solely as a love gift from God.

The most recent event in that composite picture occurred scarcely two weeks ago when I picked up the phone and heard the familiar voice of my dear friend and discipler, D. J. Warren, say, "Carol, I have something to tell you." Her precious twenty-one-year-old daughter, Sarah, had been killed by a drunk driver who was traveling on the wrong side of an Arizona highway.

Later that afternoon, we sat on the edge of her son's bed, held each other, and wept while she told me about all the *good things* God was doing in the midst of their tragedy. I freely confess my amazement at the way D. J. responded to Sarah's death. I doubt whether I would have responded that way had it been my daughter, Cinnamon. Maybe in six months or a year, but not within a few days. I found myself wondering where she found the strength.

But then I realized that she didn't "find" it. It was a love gift from her Father in heaven. When He adopted D. J. into His family, He gave her everything she would need to be spiritually strong in His service, and since that day He has been perfecting that strength in her weakness. Perfecting that strength has not been without effort on her part, however. God has required her to *work out* what He has worked in her, and she has been faithful to do so. As I look back over the years I have known her, I thank God for the powerful, God-honoring testimony of her spiritual strength.

As we embark on this study of spiritual strength, it is my prayer that God will be pleased to use it as a means of perfecting His power in our weakness, as He has in hers, so that we will become better equipped to walk worthy of our high calling in Christ.

PART 1

The Mindset of Strength

1

A Matter of Focus

The duties God requires of us are not in proportion to the strength we possess in ourselves. Rather, they are proportional to the resources available to us in Christ.
—John Owen

I am always amazed at God's timing. The weekend following Sarah Warren's death, I was scheduled to speak at a women's retreat at Prindle Pond, Massachusetts, on the topic of spiritual strength. The topic had been determined eight months before I was to speak, and I had been immersed in my subject for at least half of that time. As I watched my dear friend respond to the tragic loss of her daughter, I realized she was the perfect example of everything I planned to say about strength. I asked her for permission to use her story, and she quickly gave it, telling me that she wanted Sarah's life and death to touch as many people as possible.

As I thought about how I might best use her story to illustrate scriptural truth for the ladies in New England, I was struck by the fact that D. J.'s exemplary spiritual strength is primarily *a matter of focus.* For all the years I have known her, she has walked with her eyes fixed firmly on Christ. Her mind is set on the things above, not on the things of the earth; and she consistently seeks first God's kingdom and His righteousness in the routine affairs of her daily life.

The Heart and Soul of Spiritual Strength

My friend takes quite seriously Paul's words to the Colossians: "If then you have been raised up with Christ, keep seeking the things above, where Christ is, seated at the right hand of God. Set your mind on the things above, not on the things that are on earth" (3:1–2). And she considers herself one of the disciples to whom Jesus said, "Do not be anxious for your life. . . . for your heavenly Father knows that you need all these things. But seek first His kingdom and His righteousness; and all these things shall be added to you" (Matthew 6:25, 32–33).

Interestingly, although neither of those passages uses the word *strength,* they capture, quite eloquently and concisely, the very essence of the spiritual strength that I see in D. J. They do that by focusing our attention squarely on the only Source of spiritual strength, and by reminding us that we must consistently draw on that Source if we are to reflect our Father's purpose for our salvation.

If you have been a Christian for very long, you know that you need strength to obey God's commands. You also know that the strength you need doesn't reside within you. It has to come from an external Source—the Source Paul describes for us in the book of Colossians.

Paul wrote Colossians for the purpose of affirming the *preeminence of Christ* (Colossians 1:18 NKJV). The Christians in Colossae had fallen under the influence of false teachers who were diluting the great truths of the gospel that pointed to the preeminence of Christ in all things. Those teachers weren't necessarily denying Christ outright. They were suggesting, and in some cases boldly proclaiming, that Christ isn't enough. They were teaching a theology of "Christ-plus" something else. If that sounds familiar to you, it is most likely because that same kind of false teaching is running rampant in the church today.

Paul was incensed by that kind of teaching simply because it isn't true. He knew that the lives of the Colossian believers (and of all believers throughout the ages) had to be grounded in God's absolute truth[1] if they were to live out God's purpose for their salvation. Paul knew that when Christians allow themselves to be drawn away from God's absolute truth by listening to and believing the kinds of lies being taught in Colossae (and in the world today), they inevitably lose their ability to serve God effectively. So he encouraged them to lift their eyes from such earthly thinking and set their minds on the things above where Christ is seated at the right hand of God, *preeminently* exercising all authority and dispensing strength to His people.

Spiritual strength, therefore, is primarily a matter of focus. When we seek the things above and when our minds are set on Christ, we will be strong. But when we allow our focus to shift to the things of this earth, we will soon find ourselves growing weaker and weaker.

Will Being So Heavenly Minded Make You No Earthly Good?

Have you ever been cautioned by well-meaning Christians to *guard against being so heavenly minded, you're no earthly good?* I certainly have. And I always thought they had a good point—until I began to think deeply about Paul's admonition to the Colossians. His words "Set your mind on the things above, not on the things that are on the earth" stand in clear contradistinction to the advice most of us have been given. In Colossians 3:1–2, Paul declares that those who are the *most* heavenly minded are the very ones who are of the *most* earthly good! And his other writings clarify and support this surprising assertion.

Throughout all of his letters Paul emphasizes our high calling in Christ and exhorts us to walk worthy of that high calling. When he refers to our high calling, he is referring to God's purpose for saving us and then leaving us here on earth instead of transporting us immediately to heaven.

The Westminster Shorter Catechism summarizes God's purpose for our salvation with the words, "Man's chief end is to glorify God, and to enjoy him forever" (Q/A 1). We can accept that statement as true because the men who wrote it derived it from Scripture. God tells His children through the prophet Isaiah:

> Do not fear, for I have redeemed you;
> I have called you by name; you are Mine! . . .
> Since you are precious in My sight,
> Since you are honored and I love you . . .
> Do not fear, for I am with you;
> I will bring your offspring from the east,
> And gather you from the west.
> I will say to the north, "Give them up!"
> And to the south, "Do not hold them back."
> Bring My sons from afar,
> And My daughters from the ends of the earth,
> *Everyone who is called by My name,*
> *And whom I have created for My glory,*
> *Whom I have formed, even whom I have made . . .*
> *The people whom I have formed for Myself*
> *Will declare My praise.* (43:1, 4–7, 21)

God also uses Paul's eloquent pen to declare to the Ephesians that we have been chosen and predestined to adoption *to the praise of the glory of His grace,* that we who hope in Christ are *to the praise of His glory,* and that the Holy Spirit's seal of our redemption is also *to the praise of His glory* (1:3–14). God's Word leaves no doubt that we were created and saved to glorify Him.

But we were also created and saved to enjoy our God. In fact, we glorify Him best when we enjoy Him most.[2] The psalmist says,

> Let all who seek Thee rejoice and be glad in Thee;
> Let those who love Thy salvation say continually,
> "The LORD be magnified!" (Psalm 40:16; see also
>   16:11; 35:9, 37; 70:4).

We glorify God when we reflect His attributes accurately to those around us. Those who do that effectively will accomplish *the most earthly good* because they will fulfill their purpose as Christians. But doing that requires being heavenly minded. Paul tells us in Ephesians that God calls out His elect and equips them in Christ to do works of service during their time on the earth (2:8–10). Then he reminds us that doing those works demands being imitators of God (5:1). Of course, we cannot imitate God if we are not focused on Him.

Walking Worthy Requires Us to Be Strong

Paul knew that walking worthy of such a high calling would be difficult for us for at least two very good reasons: First, the good works God has prepared for us redeemed sinners must be done in a world full of unredeemed sinners. Therefore, those works always cut cross grain to our own natural inclinations and also to the strong cultural currents in which we live.

Second, those good works will be hatefully and violently

opposed by God's enemy Satan, who becomes our enemy too the minute we are adopted into the family of God. One well-known Bible teacher expressed this truth vividly when he said, "When a person becomes a Christian, that person is then and there declaring war on hell. And hell fights back. . . . The fainthearted and compromisers need not apply." Christians are not only called to work hard in God's service, but they are also expected to do battle with Satan.

Paul knew, from his own personal experience, that Christians have inadequate strength in themselves to accomplish God's purposes for them. Only by fixing our eyes on the exalted, preeminent Christ—not on the things of the earth—will we be able to build enough spiritual muscle to move mountains at God's command. So forget that well-meaning advice about being too heavenly minded, and take Paul's word instead: The more heavenly minded you are, the more earthly good you will be!

Building Up a Weak Church

As believers in Jesus Christ, we desperately need to pay attention to Paul, because very few Christians these days are up to the task of moving mountains at God's command. The evangelical church in our day, as a whole, is extremely weak. It is definitely having less of an impact on the world than the world is having on it!

A. W. Tozer, in his classic book on worship *The Knowledge of the Holy,* tells us why:

> The history of mankind will probably show that no people has ever risen above its religion, and man's spiritual history will positively demonstrate that no religion has ever been greater than its view of God. . . . So necessary to the Church is a lofty concept of God that when that concept in any meas-

ure declines, the Church . . . declines along with it. The first step down for any church is taken when it surrenders its high opinion of God.[3]

Here Tozer describes, in his characteristically compelling style, the need to establish and maintain a God-centered focus in the Christian life. That kind of focus is absolutely essential to a strong, effective church.

The church of Jesus Christ has grown weak as it has become more people-focused than God-focused. The church as a whole seems more interested in *attracting* the worldly by looking a lot like them than it is in *exalting* God by maintaining its distinctiveness as the people of God. We have forgotten that our *distinctiveness* is what makes us most attractive to a lost and dying world!

We are drifting away from the idea that God's gracious gifts are to be used to accomplish His purposes, His way. We are letting our minds shift from the things that are above to the things that are on the earth. And in the process, we are becoming weaker and weaker.

But we can stop the process. You and I, reader and writer, can start reversing this distressing trend this very minute. As believers in Jesus Christ, we have been given everything we need to be spiritually strong. The components, or raw materials, of spiritual strength were given to us, free of charge, by our Father God when He adopted us as His children.

He knows very well that His call to salvation is a call to action, and that walking worthy of our high calling in Christ requires us to be spiritually fit. He also knows that, in our fallen state, we do not have the resources to build the strength required for the work He has called us to do. So He gives us everything that we need to accomplish His purposes for our salvation. Of course, simply having these resources in our possession won't make us strong. Spiritual strength comes and grows only as we consistently focus on Christ and use what we have been given to do God's work, God's way. But before we can do that, we must become familiar with the tools we've been given to do that work.

A Helpful Analogy

As I watched my friend D. J. glorify God by standing strong in His might in the midst of her grief, I realized that her spiritual strength hadn't come through a sudden infusion. She had been building it, consistently and persistently, throughout her Christian life. As I thought about her example, the strength-building analogy I had planned to present to ladies at Prindle Pond sharpened its focus. Neither spiritual nor physical strength comes by sudden infusion. Both require patient development.

The remaining lessons in this "Focus" study develop an analogy between spiritual and physical strength. In lessons 2–6, we'll examine the essential components (or raw materials) of spiritual strength by comparing them to the essential components of physical strength. We will see that just as physical strength depends upon (1) physical life, (2) good solid bones, (3) sturdy muscles, (4) an efficient cardiopulmonary system, and (5) resilient skin, spiritual strength relies upon (1) spiritual life, (2) knowledge of God, (3) faith in Christ Jesus, (4) supernatural love, and the (5) fellowship that exists within the bonds of God's family.

In lessons 7–10, we'll learn that mere possession of those components does not yield strength. Rather, strength comes and grows when we put them to work in a well-designed workout routine. Just as physical strength is built up and maintained when a personal trainer guides us through a program of good nutrition, strenuous exercise, and rejuvenating rest, spiritual strength is the product of

God's Holy Spirit guiding us through a regimen of Bible intake, obedience to God, and regular prayer.

Lessons 11–13 prepare us to fight off persistent assaults of four devious strength stealers—laziness, neglect, disease, and injury, each of which saps spiritual strength just as destructively as it does physical strength.

A Few Words to Grow On

As we prepare ourselves to grow strong in the Lord, let's pause for a moment to reset our focus. Building spiritual strength is, without doubt, an arduous journey—one that will prove overwhelming if we fail to recall that we never travel alone. Paul reminds us that although *we* are required to work out our salvation, it is *God* who is at work in us both to will and to work for His good pleasure (Philippians 2:13–14). If we want to possess great spiritual strength, we need to rely on and draw courage from our brother's assurance.

Before we begin working on the exercises to lesson 1, let's meditate for a few moments on the following praise phrases written by one of God's strongest men. As you read, ponder how King David's words reflect his dependence upon the same truth Paul expressed many centuries later:

> I will love You,
>   O LORD, my strength.
> The LORD is my rock and my fortress and my
>   deliverer;
> My God, my strength,
>   in whom I will trust;
> My shield and the horn of my salvation, my
>   stronghold.
> I will call upon the LORD,
>   who is worthy to be praised;
> So shall I be saved from my enemies. . . .

For You will light my lamp;
The LORD my God will enlighten my darkness.
For by You I can run against a troop,
And by my God I can leap over a wall.
As for God, His way is perfect;
The word of the LORD is proven;
He is a shield to all who trust in Him.

For who is God, except the LORD?
And who is a rock, except our God?
It is God who arms me with strength,
And makes my way perfect. . . .

The LORD lives!
Blessed be my Rock!
Let the God of my salvation be exalted.
  (Psalm 18:1–3, 28–32, 46 NKJV)

Notes

1. Francis Schaeffer uses the phrase "true truth" to refer to this absolute, unchanging truth that comes only from God through direct revelation. (See John 4:24; 8:32; 14:6; 17:17 for scriptural affirmation and description of this kind of truth.)

2. For a deeper presentation of the ways in which our joy in God glorifies Him best, see the works of John Piper, particularly, *Desiring God* (Sisters, Ore.: Multnomah, 1996).

3. A. W. Tozer, *The Knowledge of the Holy* (San Francisco: Harper and Row, 1961), 1, 4.

Exercises

Review

1. Read Colossians 3:1–2 in the light of Psalm 18 (in its entirety), and use what you have read to support the assertion, "Spiritual strength is primarily a matter of focus."

2. Who is our only Source of spiritual strength? Explain the importance of consistently drawing on that Source. Connect the importance of consistently drawing on the only Source of spiritual strength with Paul's purpose for writing the book of Colossians.

3. Is it likely that great devotion to Christ will leave you "so heavenly minded, you're no earthly good"? Explain your answer, supporting your ideas with Scripture.

4. List at least two reasons why walking worthy of our high calling in Christ is difficult for us. What is the solution to this difficulty?

5. How do A. W. Tozer's words on pages 16–17 reveal at least one factor contributing to the weakness of the evangelical church in our day?

6. List and briefly describe the raw materials God has given us to help us build spiritual strength. What are the essential elements in an effective spiritual work-out routine? List four devious strength stealers that sap spiritual strength just as destructively as they do physical strength.

Application

1. Do you know anyone who exemplifies spiritual strength in ways similar to my friend D. J.? If so, describe how

he or she displays spiritual strength in the routine affairs of daily life. If you do not know anyone who exemplifies spiritual strength in this way, describe a character from the Bible or from church history who did. What can you learn from this person's example that will help you become a stronger Christian? Make a step-by-step plan to implement change in your life based on what you have learned from this person.

2. Describe one or more "earthly" endeavors you desire to do well (for example, job performance, parenting, a community service project, volunteer work, academic pursuits, or hobbies). Think about and then explain how being more "heavenly minded" will help you do more earthly good in the endeavor(s) you described.

3. Begin memorizing one or more of the following Scripture passages:

   Psalm 70:4
   Isaiah 43:7, 21
   Colossians 3:1–2

Digging Deeper

1. Read A. W. Tozer's book *The Knowledge of the Holy,* and write an analysis of how deepening our understanding of the character and nature of God will strengthen the evangelical church in our day. What are some ways you can encourage other Christians to begin deepening their understanding of God? When and where will you begin implementing the ways you listed?

The Components
of Strength

2

The Life of Salvation

The Church is largely wasting her time . . . in imagining that, if you give people the Christian ethic and urge them to practice it, the problems of the world will be solved. It cannot be done; regeneration is essential.

—D. Martyn Lloyd-Jones

During the years in which I taught biblical principles for living within the context of biblical counseling, I was often asked about the wisdom and propriety of counseling unbelievers with biblical principles. The discussions generated by that question were always interesting, and the issues they raised were extremely important.

Most of the Christians God calls to the ministry of biblical counseling have the gift of compassion. They earnestly desire to help hurting people. When someone they know has a problem, they want to help solve it. They are the ones to whom other people are drawn for comfort and care. They are the ones who not only are willing to listen, but always seem to have a tissue or two tucked away in their pocket.

They are also the ones who tend to question my conviction that it is usually unwise and inappropriate to counsel unbelievers with biblical principles for living. If that conviction bothers you just a bit, it's most likely because you are a highly compassionate person! *After all,* you want me to know, *biblical principles work! They will help hurting people deal with the difficulties they encounter in life.*

And you are right. Biblical principles, when diligently applied by an unbeliever, almost invariably work—and work very well—to satisfy his or her desire to deal with life's most difficult problems. But consider with me, from the perspective of Scripture, whether satisfying that unbeliever's desire through the use of biblical life principles is necessarily wise and appropriate.

God has revealed His truth through the Scriptures in order to bring His chosen children into His family and to teach them to glorify and enjoy Him during their sojourn on earth. Wise, appropriate use of the principles we find in Scripture includes a specific intent to fulfill God's purposes for them. Using them as a means of satisfying human desires that are inconsistent with God's purposes amounts to misappropriation of the resources we have been given for use in His service.

Perhaps that is why God also calls to the ministry of biblical counseling a few Christians who are short on compassion but long on discernment. Wise, appropriate use of God's Word to help hurting people is best accomplished when compassionate problem solvers join forces with those gifted to see that the *real problem* often lies buried beneath the immediate difficulty.

Strength for Life Is Irrelevant If You're Dead

Effective biblical counseling essentially entails using the truths of the Bible to infuse strength for life into the weak, the discouraged, or the completely distraught. Doing that in a way that glorifies God involves more than "solving" problems of life in an effort to help distressed people feel better. It includes helping the distressed understand and live out God's purposes for them.

Therefore, effective biblical counselors balance compassion with wisdom by using biblical principles for the ends God intended. Colossians 3:1–2 and Matthew 6:33 summarize well the thrust of that effort. Hurting people will be most effectively helped when they are encouraged to set their minds on the things above and to seek first God's kingdom and righteousness.

Wise, compassionate biblical counselors know that strength for the life God designed us to live comes from only one Source—the exalted preeminent Christ, who exercises all authority from the right hand of God. And they also know that only those who are alive in Christ Jesus can access that Source and wisely use what they find there. That is why wise, compassionate biblical counselors always begin helping the hurting by checking for signs of spiritual life. They know that even the most diligent efforts to infuse strength for life into a spiritual corpse will not produce eternal benefit.

The Life of Salvation

Spiritual life comes to us through salvation in Christ. And spiritual strength is impossible without spiritual life. If we have not been regenerated, reconciled to God, and redeemed from the power of sin, we cannot be spiritually strong. Spiritual life is essential for spiritual strength for two basic reasons: (1) it transforms us from people enslaved by the power of sin into people empowered by God's Holy Spirit to work out our salvation; and (2) it qualifies us to enter God's presence where we have access to all of His mighty resources to use in accomplishing the work He wants us to do.

Transformation occurs when God *regenerates* sinners. Regeneration is an act of re-creation by which God breathes His life into the spiritually dead. I like to think of it as "God's CPR." The American Red Cross may have taught you, as it did me, that when you encounter an unconscious person devoid of heartbeat and breath, it won't do any good to exhort them to get up. No matter how persuasive you are, they cannot respond. Without heartbeat and breath, they are officially dead. And dead people are incapable of helping themselves. Before they can act on your good advice, you must take steps to restore them to life. And if you don't know how to do that, the American Red Cross will be delighted to teach you!

In much the same way, spiritually dead sinners cannot respond to the good advice in the Bible unless God acts in His grace to restore them to spiritual life. The prophet Ezekiel describes spiritually dead sinners as those whose hearts are hard as stone. They do not respond to God's truth because their response organ is dead. No amount of persuasion will convince them to do what they are unable to do. Before they can respond to God's truth, their hearts must be quickened. Responding to God requires transformation. And the only One who is able to transform stony hearts is God Himself.

Of course, He is under no obligation to do so. He has every reason and every right to let stony hearts remain dead in their trespass and sin, but He has graciously chosen to glorify His own name by breathing life into some:

> Thus says the Lord GOD, "It is not for your sake, O house of Israel, that I am about to act, but for My holy name. . . . Then the nations will know that I am the LORD," declares the Lord GOD, "when I prove My-

self holy among you in their sight. For I will take you from the nations, gather you from all the lands, and bring you into your own land. Then I will sprinkle clean water on you, and you will be clean; I will cleanse you from all your filthiness and from all your idols. Moreover, I will give you a new heart and put a new spirit within you; and I will remove the heart of stone from your flesh and give you a heart of flesh. And I will put My Spirit within you and cause you to walk in My statutes, and you will be careful to observe My ordinances." (Ezekiel 36:22–27)

God acted to transform the ones He had chosen through the necessary work[1] of the Second Person of the Godhead. Jesus Christ, "although He existed in the form of God, did not regard equality with God a thing to be grasped," but willingly took the form of a bond-servant in His incarnation so that He could do what was required to save chosen sinners (Philippians 2:6–7).

During His life on the earth, Jesus kept God's righteous law perfectly, allowing us to be credited with its fulfillment. By His death He became sin on our behalf and paid the law's penalty so that we wouldn't have to. When He arose from the tomb on the third day, He swallowed up death in victory and defused its sting by breaking sin's power. And when He ascended to the right hand of God, He assumed all authority and poured forth the empowering Spirit upon His adopted brothers and sisters. Then He sat down to intercede for them as their perfect Advocate.

Jesus Christ's perfect life and substitutionary death *reconciled* us to God. As lost sinners, we were God's enemies, separated from Him by an impassable gulf. Christ bridged that gulf by keeping God's righteous law and then by paying the penalty for chosen lawbreakers. God reconciled us to Himself by crediting our account with Christ's obedience and by forgiving our sin based upon Jesus' payment of the debt we owed. Paul tells us that God "made Him who knew no sin to be sin on our behalf, that we might become the righteousness of God in Him" (2 Corinthians 5:21).

But our salvation in Christ doesn't stop there. It not only dealt with sin's penalty, but also broke its power. God chose to enhance His own glory by leaving His reconciled children here on the earth as *redeemed* saints of God. Redemption has to do with transfer of ownership. Paul tells us in Romans 6:14, 17–18 that sin is no longer master over us because we are no longer slaves of sin but slaves of righteousness. Ownership of our souls has been transferred from sin's sovereign, Satan, to the righteous Sovereign, almighty God. Sin's power to control us was decisively broken when Christ rose from the dead, ascended to God's right hand, assumed all power and authority, and poured forth the Spirit.

The spiritual strength that we need to work out our salvation to the glory of God is completely dependent upon our being transformed and transferred from the domain of darkness into the kingdom of God's beloved Son. If you have not yet been so transformed and transferred (or if you have any doubts about whether you have), please stop at this point, read appendix A, and ask God to breathe His life into your soul as you read.

Power for Living

God saves fallen sinners and gives them His Spirit for a very good reason. He has prepared certain "good works" for each of them to do that will glorify Him and further His kingdom. These good works exceed the bounds of human ability, which is why, along with our salvation, God also gives us power and gifts through His indwelling Spirit. God enhances His glory by accomplishing His purposes through the use of weak means. He is pleased to perfect His power in redeemed human weakness.

J. I. Packer explains it like this: "God uses us, calling into play the powers he has given us, as channels through which his own power flows. . . . It is very clear from the New Testament that the power of God is meant to accompany the gospel, and to find expression through its messenger and in the lives of those to whom the messenger comes."[2]

Those who are alive in Christ Jesus quite literally have their work cut out for them. And it doesn't take long to realize that we're too weak to do it. No matter how diligently we apply our frail human abilities, we will always fall short of God's purposes for us. If we want to walk worthy of our high calling in Christ, we must draw on His resources instead of our own.

Those divine resources are abundant, and they are at our disposal to use in the work of the kingdom. That's because our salvation *unites* us with Christ, and being united with Him gives us *access to God*. Scripture teaches that God is too holy to look upon evil and wickedness (Habakkuk 1:13). And since in our fallen state we are evil and wicked, we could not enter His presence or access His resources if we were not united with Christ in His perfect righteousness. Colossians 1:22 tells us that Christ "reconciled [us] in His fleshly body through death, in order to present [us] before Him holy and blameless and beyond reproach."

When Christ presents us before God, "holy and blameless and beyond reproach," we stand amazed in the glow of His grace, mercy, and love. We simply cannot comprehend why beings so vile and wretched would be chosen of God to accomplish His purposes. We freely acknowledge our lack of worth and ability to be used as His means in the work of the kingdom. But then we hear Him affirm His divine right to "have mercy on whom I have mercy, and . . . [to have] compassion on whom I have compassion" (Romans 9:15). And we bow in humble submission and gratitude as we understand that "it does not depend on the man who wills or the man who runs, but on God who has mercy" (v. 16).

We rejoice in the knowledge that we have been chosen "in the Beloved" to do the good works He prepared for us before time began, but we wonder where in the world we will find the resources to do them. That's when we hear Him say that those resources can't be found in the world, but only in Him. "His divine power has granted to us everything pertaining to life and godliness. . . . He has granted to us His precious and magnificent promises." "And God is able to make all grace abound to you, that always having all sufficiency in everything, you may have an abundance for every good deed" (2 Peter 1:3–4; 2 Corinthians 9:8).

Getting a good solid grip on this marvelous truth is absolutely essential for those who want to be strong in their service to God. J. I. Packer warns us that "generally speaking, our expectations with regard to seeing the power of God transforming people's lives are not as high as they should be."[3]

The first step in working out the salvation we have been given is raising our expectations of what He can and will do in us and through us when we set our minds on the things above and seek first His kingdom and righteousness. As we proceed in our study of spiritual strength, will you join me in Paul's prayer that we will

> be able to comprehend with all the saints what is the breadth and length and height and depth, and to know the love of Christ which surpasses knowledge, that [we] may be filled up to all the fulness of God. Now to Him who is able to do exceeding abundantly beyond all that we ask or think, according to the power that works within us, to Him be the glory

in the church and in Christ Jesus to all generations
forever and ever. Amen. (Ephesians 3:18–21)

Notes

1. For a deep, rich discussion of the necessity of Christ's
   work as well as its nature, see John Murray, *Redemption
   Accomplished and Applied* (Grand Rapids: Eerdmans,
   1955).

2. J. I. Packer, *Rediscovering Holiness* (Ann Arbor, Mich.: Servant, 1992), 203, 210.

3. Ibid., 212.

Exercises

Review

1. Although not all Christians are called to the "ministry"
   of biblical counseling, all Christians minister from time
   to time by trying to help those who are hurting. Explain
   why the *first step* in both cases is checking for signs of
   spiritual life.

2. What are the two basic reasons for saying that spiritual
   life is essential for spiritual strength? Can you think of
   other reasons that support that assertion? If so, list them
   also.

3. Distinguish between regeneration, reconciliation to God, and redemption from the power of sin. What part does each play in equipping sinners to be spiritually strong?

4. Describe at least four aspects of the necessary work Christ accomplished in His incarnation. How does each of these aspects glorify God? How does each benefit us?

5. Read Matthew 5:16 and Ephesians 2:8–10. Then describe the work that Christians have cut out for them. Then read 2 Corinthians 4:7–18; 11:16–12:10; and Philippians 3:11–14, and explain why God designed this work to exceed the bounds of human ability.

6. Explain how our union with Christ gives us access to God and His mighty resources. Why is grasping this truth important for Christians who want to be strong in God's service?

Application

1. Describe a time when you were in a position to "infuse strength for life" into someone who was weak, discouraged or completely distraught. How did you respond to this person? Were you confident of his or her salvation? If not, did you begin by checking for signs of spiritual life? Were you more intent upon helping this person feel better—or upon helping him or her understand and live out God's purposes? Explain your answers to these questions, using specific examples. If you were given this same opportunity now after studying lesson 2, would you do anything differently? Explain.

2. Read Romans 6, paying particular attention to verses 12–18. Is there a specific sin in your life that you be-

lieve you are too weak to overcome or control? What does Romans 6 (vv. 12–18 in particular) say about that belief? What hope do you find in these verses for overcoming or controlling this sin? Make a detailed, step by step plan to guide you in not letting this sin reign in your life. If you need help making this plan, consult with a trusted, mature Christian friend, your pastor, or one of your church leaders.

3. Review the verse(s) you began memorizing in lesson 1. Then begin memorizing one or more of the following:

   Matthew 5:16
   Romans 6:12–14
   Ephesians 2:8–10

Digging Deeper

1. Study the concept of the Christian's union with Christ. (John Murray's book, *Redemption Accomplished and Applied* is a good resource, but is not easy reading!) Then design a teaching or discipling tool based on this concept that you can use to raise the expectations of Christians you know "with regard to seeing the power of God transforming people's lives."

3

The Good Bones
of Knowledge

One of the greatest obstacles encountered in a teaching ministry is this idea, pervasive in the Christian Church, that there is no benefit to be had by the laity in serious study of the Word of God or in the study of theology. We have elevated to the level of an ideal, the idea of having a simple childlike faith. . . . There is a close connection between simplicity and naïveté. Believers who have not been deeply trained and matured in the things of God, are vulnerable and exposed to every wind of doctrine that blows through the Church. . . . We are exposed to these things and vulnerable to them because we simply do not have a mature understanding of the truth of God.   —R. C. Sproul

Around two o'clock on the morning of Sunday, October 31, 1999, EgyptAir Flight 990 inexplicably plunged thirty-three thousand feet into the Atlantic off the coast of Nantucket. None of the 217 people on board survived.

At the moment their souls plummeted into eternity, I was

sound asleep in a motel room overlooking the lake in beautiful downtown Burlington, Ontario. When I heard about the disaster later that day, I was shocked and horrified—not only by the tragedy itself, but also by the spiritual weakness reflected in my very first thoughts.

You see, I was scheduled to fly home to Albuquerque the very next day—and I thought I had gotten a grip on my fear of flying. But I found myself seriously considering forfeiting my plane ticket and renting a car to drive home! Yes, I realized the great distance involved, but getting back on an airplane suddenly seemed like an impossible feat. My stomach was churning, my mouth was dry, and my hands were like ice. Every thought in my mind had been taken captive by fear.

Although deep in my soul I realized that I wouldn't actually rent a car to drive home, I was terrified by the mere thought of four hours on airplanes. *How in the world would I get through that ordeal without completely blowing my witness?* Then God's Holy Spirit reminded me that I would *not* honor Him in it as long as my thoughts remained fixed on the things *in the world*. I had to fix them firmly on Christ. And there was only one sure way to do that: by reminding myself of what I knew about God.

Knowledge Is Power

As I grabbed my Bible and headed toward an inviting bench on the shore of the lake, I recalled hearing R. C. Sproul remark, on one of his tapes, that fear is an essential ingredient of courage—because if you're not afraid, you're not acting in courage. *Well, I've certainly got that part nailed down,* I thought as I opened my little red "travel Bible" to the first chapter of Joshua.

I wanted Joshua's company on my lakeside bench because I think he was as frightened as I was by the required journey before him. He had stepped into Moses' oversized shoes, and now stood on the edge of God's Promised Land. He had heard God command him to lead Israel into that land to conquer and possess it, and the time had come to obey that command. Joshua had already demonstrated his great faith in God, but I believe that in spite of his great faith, he may well have been shaking in Moses' shoes as he stood there that day.

What makes me think a trained warrior like Joshua was as scared as I was? Because of the words that our omniscient God spoke to him while he stood there.

> Moses My servant is dead; now therefore arise, cross this Jordan, you and all this people, to the land which I am giving to them, to the sons of Israel. . . . No man will be able to stand before you all the days of your life. Just as I have been with Moses, I will be with you; I will not fail you or forsake you. Be strong and courageous, for you shall give this people possession of the land which I swore to their fathers to give them. Only be strong and very courageous; be careful to do according to all the law which Moses My servant commanded you; do not turn from it to the right or to the left, so that you may have success wherever you go. This book of the law shall not depart from your mouth, but you shall meditate on it day and night, so that you may be careful to do according to all that is written in it; for then you will make your way prosperous, and then you will have success. Have I not commanded you? Be strong and courageous! Do not tremble or be dismayed, for the LORD your God is with you wherever you go. (Joshua 1:2, 5–9)

Did you notice the way God reminds Joshua repeatedly to "be strong and courageous!"? That's the kind of advice people give to someone who is scared. Did you also notice that God's reminders don't take the form of ego-bolstering pep-talks? It's interesting that God doesn't say, *C'mon Joshua. You can do this! You're a born leader. You're a trained warrior. You've watched Moses work. It's gonna be a piece a' cake once you get moving. So gird up those loins, and just do it!*

Rather, God focuses His servant's thoughts firmly on Him when He says, in effect: *Joshua, I have promised this land to the people of Israel, and I am going to give it to them. No one who currently lives in the land will be able to stop the accomplishment of My plans. Because you know Me well enough to trust Me, you can be strong and courageous in the task I have given you. Set your mind on My truth, revealed in My law. Don't deviate from it one iota. Memorize it and think about it all day and all night. That's what it takes to be successful in My service. You know I am going with you as you enter the land, and that I have promised never to leave you or forsake you; therefore, I command you to be strong and courageous!*

As you look over Joshua's shoulder with me, can you see how *knowledge of God and His purposes* infuses strength for kingdom service into His chosen children? It does that by protecting, supporting, and giving form to our spiritual lives, in much the same way that good solid bones protect, support, and give form to our physical bodies.

The Good Bones of Knowledge

If you've studied human anatomy and physiology, you know that good solid bones contribute a great deal to the health and well-being of our physical bodies. And of course, the most obvious benefits of good solid bones are their ability to provide recognizable form to a physical being, and to support and protect other bodily structures.

If you happen to dig up a skeleton in your backyard

while preparing your garden, you can quickly surmise whether what died there was a chipmunk, a cat, a horse, or a person. And if you'll activate your imagination with me for a moment, you'll be able to picture the wimpy-limp state we'd be in if all of our bones suddenly melted into our shoes!

If we want to be physically strong, we must build and maintain good solid bones. And if we want to be spiritually strong, we must build and maintain the good bones of knowledge. That's because knowledge of God and His purposes protects, supports, and gives form to our service to God.

I learned that lesson well as I sat with Joshua by the lake and pondered God's truth about frightening journeys. I must admit that when I heard the news about the EgyptAir crash, every spiritual bone in my body suddenly seemed to melt into my shoes. I felt unprotected, wimpy-limp, and completely unrecognizable as a bold, confident Christian.

However, as providence would have it, the very weekend before, I had taught sixty-four ladies at a retreat that knowledge of God and His purposes forms the essential skeleton of spiritual strength. My distressingly weak response to God-ordained circumstances made me ask myself whether I had been listening to what I was saying. It was time for a review!

Say It Again, Paul

I turned to the passage I had used with those ladies: Colossians 1:9–12, one of Paul's most powerful intercessory prayers. The apostle had just finished commending the Colossians for the quality of their faithful service to God, when he launched into this description of the way he and Timothy had been praying for them. Listen carefully to the kind of prayer requests they routinely made for the believers at Colossae.

> For this reason also, since the day we heard of it, we have not ceased to pray for you and to ask that you may be filled with the knowledge of His will in all spiritual wisdom and understanding, so that you may walk in a manner worthy of the Lord, to please Him in all respects, bearing fruit in every good work and increasing in the knowledge of God; strengthened with all power, according to His glorious might, for the attaining of all steadfastness and patience; joyously giving thanks to the Father, who has qualified us to share in the inheritance of the saints in light.

What was the first thing Paul requested from God for the Colossians? That they *may be filled with the knowledge of God's will in all spiritual wisdom and understanding*. Is that the first thing you request for the people for whom you pray? It should be—because wise, insightful knowledge of God's will protects, supports, and gives form to every aspect of our lives in Christ Jesus. I can't think of anything the people for whom we pray need more than that.

Paul's very next phrase explains the primary reason we need wise insightful knowledge of God's will for us. *So that [we] can walk in a manner worthy of the Lord*. Walking worthy of our high calling in Christ demands that we work hard at fulfilling His purposes for us. Doing that work successfully requires us to know what His purposes are and to know Him well enough to confidently trust Him in all situations.

Although God does not reveal to us complete, exhaustive knowledge of Himself and His purposes, He tells us all that we need to boldly obey Him (see Deuteronomy 29:29). He also gives us His indwelling Spirit to help us understand what He has told us and to wisely apply it in our daily lives. When we act in accord with such insightful knowledge, we do His will for us and thus walk worthy of our high calling.

When we walk worthy of our high calling in Christ,

Paul's prayer affirms that we will please God in all respects, bear fruit in every good work, and increase our knowledge of Him. In other words, acting upon our cognitive knowledge of God's will for us works out God's purposes for our salvation at the same time it deepens our experiential knowledge of Him. This deepening experiential knowledge of God builds our confidence in Him, which in turn enhances both our desire and our ability to serve Him well. Thus, the more we know about God, both cognitively and experientially, the more effectively we do the work that He designed us to do.

Paul affirms this fact in the next verse of his prayer when he says that deep knowledge of God *strengthens* us for the purpose of steadfastly and patiently pursuing our service to God *with all power, according to His glorious might*. This statement has been worded so carefully that it deserves our close scrutiny. Notice that Paul (writing under the influence of God's Holy Spirit) chose the phrase *according to* rather than *out of* when referring to "His glorious might"? That distinction is extremely important and is easier illustrated than it is defined.

Let's say you are in charge of fund-raising for your favorite charity, and you finally work up the courage to go to a local billionaire to ask for a donation. If he invites you in and writes you out a check for one hundred dollars, he is giving to you *out of* his riches. But if he writes you a check for one million dollars, he is giving *according to* his riches.

Do you now see why Paul was inspired to choose the phrase that he did? Knowledge of God and His will strengthens us *according to* God's glorious might, not *out of it*. God is overwhelmingly generous with resources to get His work done. Paul makes that very clear in 2 Corinthians 9:8: "And God is able to make all grace abound to you, that always having all sufficiency in everything, you may have an abundance for every good deed."

God doesn't hide Himself or His will from His children. He has given us, in His revelation and through His Spirit, *everything* we need for life and godliness (2 Peter 1:3). And because He deals with us like that, our service to Him flows, not from grudging compulsion, but from joyous thanksgiving to "the Father who has qualified [us] to share in the inheritance of the saints in light."

Knowledge of God strengthens us according to His glorious might because it gives us the ability to look at every situation of life from God's perspective instead of the world's. The more we know about God and His purposes, the better equipped we will be to fix our eyes on the things above where Christ is sovereignly, preeminently exercising His full authority, instead of on the things of the earth that are passing away.

Being strong and courageous becomes almost second nature when we possess the confident knowledge that there is indeed no one like the God who has declared

> . . . the end from the beginning
> And from ancient times things which have not
>   been done,
> Saying, "My purpose will be established,
> And I will accomplish all My good pleasure."
>   (Isaiah 46:10)

Desire Springs from Need

Knowledge of God and His purposes is one of the components of spiritual strength that God gives to us free of charge when He adopts us into His family. Everything that we need to know to serve Him well is contained in His Word. However, absorbing that knowledge so that we can use it to walk worthy of our high calling in Christ doesn't come through osmosis. Because we are by nature weak, fallen sinners, we have to work at it. Proverbs 2:1–5 describes that work beautifully:

> My son, if you will receive my sayings,
> And treasure my commandments within you,
> Make your ear attentive to wisdom,
> Incline your heart to understanding;
> For if you cry for discernment,
> Lift your voice for understanding;
> If you seek her as silver,
> And search for her as for hidden treasures;
> Then you will discern the fear of the LORD,
> And discover the knowledge of God.

The effort required to accomplish such work is motivated by strong desire. Before we will work hard at understanding and applying God's Word in our lives, we must want to do so *more* than we want to do most other things. Interestingly, the apostle Peter commands us to desire deep knowledge of God and His will: "Like newborn babes, *long for* the pure milk of the word, that by it you may grow in respect to salvation" (1 Peter 2:2). Now, if you're wondering how Peter expects us to work up desires *on command,* perhaps the following true story will be of some help to you.

Following the liberation of Palestine during World War I, a force of Allied troops pursued the retreating Turks across the desert rapidly enough to outdistance their water-carrying camel train. Soon after pushing northward from Beersheba, and having been without water for some time, men began to suffer headaches, dizziness, and faintness. Before long their mouths dried up, their lips swelled and turned purple, and many began to see mirages. If they failed to reach and liberate the wells at Sheriah from enemy forces before nightfall, thousands would die.

After a successful battle at Sheriah, the strongest troops

had to wait, within twenty feet of the huge stone cisterns containing thousands of gallons of water, while the wounded and those on guard duty slaked their thirst first. Although consumed by their overwhelming desire for water, many of the strongest men had to wait almost four hours for their turn to drink.

One of the officers who witnessed that desperate march reportedly made this spiritual application: "I believe that we all learned our first real Bible lesson on the march from Beersheba to Sheriah Wells. If such were our thirst for God, for righteousness and for His will in our lives, a consuming, all-embracing, preoccupying desire, how rich in the fruit of the Spirit would we be?"[1]

Obviously, every man waiting for water that day earnestly desired to drink from those nearby stone cisterns. And it isn't difficult for us to understand that their strong desire for that water resulted from recognition of their *great need* for it.

How much more should our great need for strength in God's service instill within us a continual thirst for a deep and refreshing knowledge of Him?

Notes

1. E. M. Blaiklock, "Water," *Eternity* (August, 1966), 27, quoted in John F. MacArthur, *The Pillars of Christian Character* (Wheaton, Ill.: Crossway, 1998), 36.

Exercises

Review

1. Read Joshua 1:1–11, and use God's words to Joshua to help you explain how knowledge of God and His pur-

poses infuses strength and courage into His children. In your answer, be sure to indicate why *knowledge of God and His purposes* is more encouraging than ego-bolstering pep talks.

2. In your own words, describe several ways in which knowledge of God and His purposes functions analogously to strong healthy bones in the human body.

3. What was the first thing that Paul and Timothy requested in prayer for the Colossians? Why did they elevate this particular request to the primary position in their prayers?

4. If you did not do so in review question 3, explain how wise understanding of God's will equips us to walk worthy of our high calling in Christ.

5. Explain the significance of Paul's use of the phrase "according to" in Colossians 1:11. Use a concordance to find other verses in which Paul uses this same phrase. Does it seem to carry the same significance in those verses also?

6. What generates strong desire for knowledge of God and His purposes? Give one or more reasons why we should work at generating this kind of desire.

Application

1. Read Joshua 1:1–11 once again. Then describe how God's words to Joshua can infuse you with strength and courage in the midst of a specific real life situation. Consider the following questions in formulating your answer:

   a. What task that are you currently facing seems frightening, overwhelming, or beyond your abilities?

   b. Do you believe God has called or requires you to accomplish this task? Why?

   c. What do you know about God and His purposes that will strengthen you to accomplish this task? (Give Scripture references.)

   d. What specific actions do you need to take to accomplish this task?

   e. When and where will you begin to take these steps?

2. Read Proverbs 2:1–5 and 1 Peter 2:2, and examine yourself in their light. Do you work hard at absorbing knowledge of God and His purposes? Is your desire for God's Word as all-consuming as was the thirst of the men standing in line at Sheriah Wells? If you answered yes, describe the needs you have recognized in your life that motivate your desire. If you answered no, ask God in prayer to reveal your great need to you.

3. Review the verses you memorized in lessons 1 and 2. Then begin memorizing one or more of the following:

   Joshua 1:8–9
   Isaiah 46:9–10
   Colossians 1:9–12
   1 Peter 2:1–3

Digging Deeper

1. Refute the fallacies in the following line of reasoning: "A simple childlike faith is highly commendable for the laity; therefore, serious study of Scripture and theology holds no real benefit for them." Support your assertions with Scripture.

4

The Muscles of Faith

Faith is not a blind thing; for faith begins with knowledge. It is not a speculative thing; for faith believes facts of which it is sure. It is not an impractical, dreamy thing; for faith trusts and stakes its destiny upon the truth of revelation . . . Faith is believing that Christ is what He is said to be, and that He will do what He has promised to do, and then expecting this of Him.

—Charles Spurgeon

A few weeks ago, my friend Lisa forwarded an e-mail message to me "just in case I hadn't seen it." I hadn't and was delighted she sent it, because it added another sparkling facet to my ongoing study of spiritual strength. The message had originated with a woman who attends Wedgwood Baptist Church in Fort Worth, Texas, and detailed a bit of what God has been doing there in the past few months.

You may recall that on September 15, 1999, a gunman entered that church, killed seven people, wounded seven others, and then took his own life. The e-mail message highlighted ways in which God's grace and mercy were displayed during the attack, as well as ways in which He has sovereignly used that tragic occurrence to accomplish His purposes.

The woman described how the gunman had walked past a church playground that would have been filled with children, had not every class been running late on that particular day. She reported that he fired more than one hundred bullets into a crowd of over four hundred people and hit only fourteen. A pipe bomb that he threw into the crowd failed to explode, and sixty-plus unfired bullets were found on his body.

The seven who died were all bold Christians who passionately proclaimed their faith in Christ; however, none of the adults who were killed had children to raise. The first 911 call came in over a police radio, which reduced the response time of emergency personnel. And one of the men in the church at the time of the attack was a paramedic who used his skills to control bleeding and stabilize the injured before EMS crews arrived.

Children's leaders in other areas of the building were able to usher their students to safety without exposing them to the bloodshed. And even though some of those leaders had children in other parts of the building, including teens in the sanctuary, every leader stayed with the class for which he or she was responsible.

Since the attack, the saints at Wedgwood Baptist Church have seized upon the publicity surrounding their painful circumstances to extol God's sovereign care and to proclaim the gospel. The e-mail message I received noted numerous "open doors" for the Word through which the pastor of the church, lay members, and teens have boldly stepped to testify of their faith. Reports of conversions have come back to the church from as far away as Saudi Arabia.

The woman who originated the e-mail report closed by proclaiming her joy that God's plan to receive glory through the salvation of sinners was magnified through the events that occurred at her church. She praised God for His power displayed in the working out of His purposes, and for the comfort and strength He had dispensed to His people. Then she called upon every Christian who read her message to further magnify God's glory through the "living sacrifice" of a life wholly committed to worship and service.

As I finished reading her words, I found myself admiring her spiritual muscles—as well as those of her brothers and sisters at Wedgwood Baptist Church. These are strong saints who obviously understand that, without the muscles of faith, the good bones of knowledge hang limp and powerless, accomplishing little of worth in kingdom service.

The Muscles of Faith

As important as good solid bones are to our bodies, they cannot act on their own. Unless they team up with strong, healthy muscles, they are doomed to remain completely immobile. In much the same way, the good bones of knowledge require activation by the muscles of faith before they will benefit us very much as we strive to walk worthy of our high calling in Christ.

A. W. Pink describes this working relationship well when he says,

> The Word of God is the *objective* foundation on which my hope rests, but faith provides a *subjective* foundation, for it convinces me of the certainty of them. Faith and confidence are inseparable; just so far as I am counting upon the ability and fidelity of the Promiser, shall I be confident of receiving the things promised and which I am expecting.[1]

Objective knowledge of God and His purposes lays the indispensable foundation of spiritual strength by acquainting us with the absolute truth regarding God's nature, His work, and His promises to us. But it is subjective faith (convinced, assured belief) in God's power and reliability that stimulates trust and motivates action.

Faith functions this way because it is another love gift we receive from our Father when He adopts us into His family. Faith is *not* "our contribution to our salvation." Nor is it "our part in working out our sanctification." Paul tells us in Ephesians 2:8–9 that we are saved by grace through faith, and that *all of salvation* is a gift of God. He emphasizes that no part of salvation is "of ourselves," because if it were, we would have good reason to boast.

Paul reveals the need for God's sovereign action in our salvation when he paraphrases Psalm 14:1–3 for the believers at Rome:

> There is none righteous, not even one;
> There is none who understands,
> There is none who seeks for God;
> All have turned aside, together they have become
>   useless;
> There is none who does good,
> There is not even one. (Romans 3:10–12)

Paul's words give us several reasons why unsaved sinners do not contribute "the faith to believe" or even "the faith to receive" their own salvation: (1) they are not righteous; (2) they do not understand; (3) they do not seek God; (4) they have turned aside to become useless; and (5) they do not do what is good. *Not even one of them.* They don't contribute faith to the transaction because they can't contribute what they don't have. We know they don't have it because (1) faith is righteous, (2) faith understands, (3) faith seeks for God, (4) faith is useful, and (5) faith does what is good. Paul's words to the Romans teach us that the faith required to respond to God's call to salvation is His *gift* to those He has chosen.

God's gift of faith goes right on giving after we're saved by equipping us to *live out* God's purposes for our salvation. We can't come up with the faith to serve God any more than we can the faith to be saved. That, too, is a love gift from our Father. However, that doesn't justify irresponsible living. God requires us to use His great gift wisely and well.

Paul told the Philippians to *work out* their salvation *because* God was at work in them "to will and to work for His good pleasure" (2:12–13). And he assured the Corinthians (who were clearly having difficulty working out their salvation) that their faith would enable them to be alert, stand firm, act like men, and be strong (1 Corinthians 16:13). Apparently those troubled saints got the message, because in his second inspired letter to them, Paul expresses his joy that they are now standing firm in their faith (2 Corinthians 1:24).

A Perfect Definition of Faith

What is this faith that not only saves us, but also equips us to walk worthy of our high calling in Christ? A. W. Pink says that it is "not a blind reliance on the Word of God, but an intelligent persuasion of its veracity, wisdom, [and] beauty."[2] The great Puritan teacher Thomas Manton describes it as "the mother of obedience."[3] John Murray adds that "faith is a whole-souled act of loving trust and self-commitment."[4] And Alexis de Tocqueville reminds us that "in Ages of Faith, the final aim of life is placed beyond life."[5]

All of these definitions capture the heart and soul of biblical faith. They depict the faith we are given by our Father God as the ultimate motivator. Faith fixes our eyes on the things above and stimulates us to put our knowledge of God to work in our daily lives. But as good as these definitions are, they are not perfect. For the last word on what this saving, motivating faith is, we must look to God's revelation in Scripture.

In Hebrews 11:1, we find the perfect definition of faith: "Now faith is the assurance of things hoped for, the conviction of things not seen" (11:1). What a marvelous statement! I am always amazed at the way Scripture packs so much meaning into so few words. Most of us (particularly writers and speakers) do just the opposite. We pack so little meaning into so many words.

The writer of Hebrews doesn't do that, however, because he writes under the inspiration of God's Holy Spirit. Thus, he concisely boils down "the muscles of faith" to two basic elements: assurance and conviction. As I pondered this perfect definition of faith, I was struck by how very pragmatic it is. In fact, many commentators on Hebrews have said that these words are more of a description of faith than a definition.

One of the best of those commentators, A. W. Pink, indicates that the nature of faith lends itself better to description than to definition. Faith, he says, is not passive but active, energetic, vigorous, and fruitful. Therefore, "a life of faith is an intensely practical thing, consisting of very much more than day-dreaming, or being regaled with joyous emotions, or even resting in orthodox views of the truth."[6]

Faith acts the way it does because it fills believers with *certain assurance* of their hope in Christ and solid conviction that God's revealed truth is reliable. The faith God gives His children is a faith that is *certain* that all of His promises and pronouncements will come to pass. It knows God has sovereignly determined the end from the beginning and will accomplish all His good pleasure (Isaiah 46:9–10). The Christian's faith in God's Word is even more certain than that of a scientist who fully expects an apple dropped out of a window to fall *down* and not up.

That is why faith is so closely connected with hope in the Scriptures. The assurance of faith rests confidently in the power and truthfulness of the One who has spoken. Because we know, both objectively and experientially, that He is uniquely trustworthy, we have hope in this life regardless of circumstances. A. W. Pink expresses it like this: "Faith believes God and relies upon His veracity: as it does so, the heart is anchored and remains steady, no matter how fierce the storm, nor how protracted the season of waiting."[7]

Israel's King David exhorts us to *make use* of the faith we've been given when he describes God as a reliable refuge, a rock, and an impregnable fortress; extols His goodness, loving kindness, and care; and then concludes with these words:

> O love the LORD, all you His godly ones!
> The LORD preserves the faithful,
> And fully recompenses the proud doer.
> Be strong, and let your heart take courage,
> All you who hope in the LORD. (Psalm 31:23–24)

We can heed David's words because of faith's solid conviction that God's truth is reliable. Our faith in Christ isn't anchored in a lemon-cream pie in the sky by-and-by. Rather, it is solidly moored to the rock of divine revelation. It is perfectly rational and realistic because it comes from the Author of reason and the Creator of all. Faith so assured and so convicted generates movement!

Moving the Muscles of Faith

You know, as I do, that moving our physical muscles keeps them in good working order. If you have ever been "laid up" for long by an illness or injury, you may recall the weakness you felt when you got back on your feet. Physical muscles weaken and atrophy when they are not used—and spiritual muscles do too. If we want to be strong and courageous in kingdom service, we must make sure that our spiritual muscles get plenty of exercise.

The writer of Hebrews understood the importance of using our spiritual muscles. Following his masterful description of faith, he provides more than a dozen examples of how it can be exercised. Then he encourages his readers to get up and get moving!

> Therefore, since we have so great a cloud of witnesses surrounding us, let us also lay aside every encumbrance, and the sin which so easily entangles us, and let us run with endurance the race that is set before us, fixing our eyes on Jesus, the author and perfecter of faith, who for the joy set before Him endured the cross, despising the shame, and has sat down at the right hand of the throne of God. For consider Him who has endured such hostility by sinners against Himself, so that you may not grow weary and lose heart. (Hebrews 12:1–3)

Do you see in this exhortation to first-century Hebrew Christians the same principle Paul emphasized in Colossians 3:1–2? The principle that tells us that spiritual strength is primarily a matter of focus? All the exemplary saints whose deeds are recounted in Hebrews 11 were strong and courageous in faith because they worked out their salvation with their eyes fixed on the exalted, preeminent Jesus Christ. Their minds were not set on the things of this earth, but on the things above. The final aim of their lives was placed beyond life.

Pause and Reflect

When you read Hebrews 11, do you see yourself in the company of the bold saints described in it? Could your name be added to their spiritually strong number? If you don't think so, may I remind you that your Father gave you *the very same faith* He gave each of them? And may I suggest that we pray together this insightful, convicting Puritan prayer and allow it to stimulate us to get up and get moving!

> Teach me to behold my creator
> > his ability to save,
> > his arms outstretched,
> > his heart big for me.
> May I confide in his power and love,
> > commit my soul to him without reserve,
> > bear his image, observe his laws, pursue his
> > > service,
> > and be through time and eternity
> > > a monument to the efficacy of his grace,
> > > a trophy of his victory.
> Make me willing to be saved in his way,
> > perceiving nothing in myself, but all in Jesus:
> Help me not only to receive him but
> > to walk in him,
> > depend upon him,
> > commune with him,
> > be conformed to him,
> > follow him,
> > > imperfect, but still pressing forward,
> > > not complaining of labour, but valuing
> > > > rest,
> > > not murmuring under trials, but
> > > > thankful for my state.
> *Give me that faith which is the means of salvation;*
> *and the principle and medium of all godliness;*

> May I be saved by grace through faith.
> live by faith,
> feel the joy of faith,
> do the work of faith.
> Perceiving nothing in myself, may I find in Christ,
> wisdom, righteousness, sanctification,
> redemption.[8]

Notes

1. A. W. Pink, *An Exposition of Hebrews* (Grand Rapids: Baker, 1954), 650. Emphasis in the original.

2. Ibid., 654.

3. Thomas Manton, *James.* The Crossway Classic Commentaries, ed. Alister McGrath and J. I. Packer (Wheaton, Ill.: Crossway, 1995), 39.

4. John Murray, *Redemption Accomplished and Applied* (Grand Rapids: Eerdmans, 1955), 86.

5. Quoted in Os Guinness, *The Call: Finding and Fulfilling the Central Purpose of Your Life* (Nashville: Word, 1998), 6.

6. Pink, *Exposition of Hebrews,* 894.

7. Ibid., 650.

8. Arthur Bennett, ed. *The Valley of Vision: A Collection of Puritan Prayers and Devotions* (Carlisle, Pa.: Banner of Truth, 1975), 37. Emphasis added.

Exercises

Review

1. Describe several ways in which the saints at Wedgwood Baptist flexed their spiritual muscles during the well-publicized tragedy that occurred at their church. Do you know other Christians who have responded in similar ways to very difficult circumstances? If so, describe how they flexed their spiritual muscles also. In what ways does their example encourage you to build up your spiritual muscles?

2. Describe the relationship between the muscles of faith and the good bones of knowledge.

3. Read Romans 2:17–3:18 and Ephesians 2:1–10 carefully. Then explain the following statement: "Faith is not our contribution to our salvation; nor is it our part in working out our sanctification." Be sure to include in your explanation a description of what our responsibilities are in regard to the faith we have been given.

4. According to Hebrews 11:1, what are the two basic elements of faith? Explain the role each of these elements plays in the exercise of faith, including the ways in which they relate to each other.

5. If you didn't do so in review exercise 4, describe the connection between faith and hope.

6. Use the analogy between physical muscles and faith to explain the importance of using the faith God has given us.

Application

1. During your devotional time this week, read Hebrews 11 and pray the great Puritan prayer recorded on pages 57–58.

2. Read Hebrews 11:1–12:3. List at least ten examples of ways in which biblical characters exercised faith in their daily lives. Now list one or more ways in which you have exercised faith in your daily life within the past year. How do the "Hebrews 11 examples" encourage you to exercise your faith more strenuously? Thinking about the following questions will help you formulate your answer:

   a. Who among the Hebrews 11 examples appeals to you greatly? Why?
   b. What situations or circumstances are you facing currently that require you to exercise faith?
   c. Does the Hebrews 11 example you selected model specific behavior that you need to imitate in order to honor God in the situations or circumstances you are currently facing? If so, describe both the exemplified behavior and how you will imitate it. If not, select another example who does.
   d. What scriptural passages provide you with the knowledge about God and His purposes that you need in order to exercise faith in these situations and circumstances? (Use a concordance if necessary to find relevant passages.)
   e. What evidence do you have (both objective and experiential) that God can be trusted in these situations or circumstances? How does this evidence give you "assurance of things hoped for"?
   f. What specific actions must you take to exercise faith in these situations or circumstances?

g. When will you begin to take these actions?
h. Who loves you enough to encourage you and hold you accountable for following through on your commitment to exercise faith? When and where will you ask him or her to help you?

3. Review your memory verses from lessons 1–3, and begin memorizing one or more of the following:

Philippians 2:12–13
Hebrews 11:1–3
Hebrews 12:1–3

Digging Deeper

1. Use a concordance and other reliable study tools to research the doctrine of the total depravity of man. Then relate what you have learned to the following statement made in this lesson: "Faith is not our contribution to our salvation; nor is it our part in working out our sanctification." In what practical ways might you use your analysis of this issue to help other believers strengthen their good bones of knowledge and muscles of faith?

5

The Blood of Love

Love framed by truth is the surest verification of the power of God at work in a person. —J. I. Packer

I hope you won't think that my personality is gruesomely twisted when I tell you that I am fascinated by blood. It's not that I sit transfixed through gory movies. Rather I stand in awe of the way God designed human blood to sustain life in our bodies.

Ever since I first studied biology as a high school sophomore, I have been captivated by the intricate precision with which our cardiovascular and pulmonary systems support every bodily function. They operate as a perfectly choreographed team to deliver the oxygen essential for life's activities and to dispose of the deadly carbon dioxide produced by metabolic processes.

I'm sure you are aware that when physical muscles are deprived of their blood supply, they soon lose their strength. Muscle development and function depend upon consistent deliveries of oxygen and regular removal of carbon dioxide. When that process breaks down, muscles cease functioning.

In much the same way, well-functioning faith depends on a good love supply. That's because love acts in our souls in much the same way as blood does in our bodies. It fuels faith's activities while removing the waste products produced by spiritual metabolism.

Now in case you've forgotten a bit of your high school biology, allow me to remind you that metabolism is a chemical process in living organisms that creates growth and produces energy. The transportation services provided by blood are extremely important in that critical life process. And as we work through this lesson, we'll see that spiritual metabolism (production of spiritual growth and energy) leans just as heavily on the work done by love in the body of Christ.

A Crazy Little Thing Called Love

"Love" is one of the most overused and ill-defined words in the English language. Ask any ten people what love is, and you'll probably get twelve different answers. However, the Greek language in which the New Testament was written is much more precise when it speaks of love. It uses at least four different words to capture significant aspects of this critical concept. *Storgē* describes the emotional bond between family members. *Eros* describes the physical attraction and desire between men and women. *Phileō* describes warm, friendly affection toward people or objects. And *agapē* describes self-sacrificial action motivated by willful intent, even when the object of love is undeserving or unappreciative.

Interestingly, *storgē*[1] and *eros* are not used in the New Testament, and *phileo* is used only occasionally. The most frequently used biblical word for love is *agapē*—the kind of love that is more action than emotion and is therefore the love that works hard to support spiritual metabolism.

This kind of love is another gift we receive from our Father God when He adopts us into His family. It is the love with which He first loved us and with which He instructs us to love one another (see 1 John 4:7–21). But like the other great gifts we receive at salvation, it also comes with great responsibilities. We are required not to neglect this kind of love, but to apply ourselves diligently in using it well.

Love Motivates Faith

In reading through some of Paul's letters this week, I was struck by his reference in Galatians 5:6 to "faith working through love" as a stimulant to obedience. I took a moment to look up the Greek word translated "love" in that passage and was not surprised to discover that it was *agapē*. That tells me that love motivates faith to obey God's commands in much the same way that faith motivates knowledge to practice the truth.

Jesus told His disciples, "If you love Me, you will keep My commandments" (John 14:15), and He commanded them to "love one another, even as I have loved you. . . . By this all men will know that you are My disciples, if you have love for one another" (John 13:34–35). Loving others is never as easy as is loving Jesus, but our love for Him stimulates us to obey that command. If God had not given us love for Jesus, I suspect that our faith would just sit there, not moving a muscle.

Obeying the commands we find in God's Word is usually difficult. God's standards are unattainably high (perfection!), and His demands are frequently overwhelming or frightening. We read them and know we are too weak in ourselves to comply. As fallen, depraved creatures, we have neither the will nor the ability to walk worthy of our high calling in Christ.

However, God does more than command our obedience.

He also equips us to do what He requires. He gives us knowledge of Him and His purposes, which quickens understanding and sparks desire. He gives us faith, which builds confident trust. And then He fills us with love, which spurs us to action. First John 4:16–18 describes what God's gift of love does for His children:

> And we have come *to know and have believed* the love which God has for us. God is love, and the one who abides in love abides in God, and God abides in him. By this, love is perfected with us, that we may *have confidence* in the day of judgment; because as He is, so also are we in this world. There is no fear in love; but perfect love *casts out fear,* because fear involves punishment, and the one who fears is not perfected in love.

Although the specific context of these verses has to do with final judgment, we can certainly apply the principle taught here to all situations of life. Since "perfect love" casts out fear of judgment because it is grounded in revealed knowledge and produces confident trust in God, it will also cast out any other fears we may have in obeying His Word.

Phillip Keller captures this action-oriented, faith-fueling aspect of *agapē* when he says,

> The love of God, contrary to what most Christians think, is not some sweet, sentimental emotion that seeps into their lives from God's Spirit. The love of Christ is a powerful, profound setting of man's will to do God's will in this wretched world. It is that tough and uncompromising determination of a man's entire soul to submit to God's Spirit in complying with His wishes and carrying out His commands.[2]

Love Also Cleans Up Faith's Debris

God's love shed abroad in our hearts certainly energizes the actions of faith. But it doesn't stop there. It also works hard at cleaning up the debris that is produced by all that activity. Now, if the idea that faith working in love produces debris sounds strange to you, remember that we exercise faith in love as fallen creatures. Therefore, even our very best faithful efforts will generate some "relational waste"— things like irritation, hard feelings and hurt feelings, jealousy, misunderstanding, anger, animosity, and even hatred. If you spend any time at all around other people (even other Christians), you know what I'm talking about. But love also deals with that relational waste.

The apostle Peter emphasized this function of love when he encouraged believers to "keep fervent in [their] love for one another, because love covers a multitude of sins" (1 Peter 4:8). One insightful biblical commentator paraphrased Peter's words in this memorable statement: "Love bears, but it never bares." Love persists consistently with other people, while striving to protect them in the process. And those loving actions clean up a lot of relational waste!

How Does Love Do It?

Christian love operates the way it does because it flows from God the Father to His chosen children through the power of His Holy Spirit with the intent of accomplishing God's purposes for their salvation. God's children draw on their knowledge of Him to exercise the faith necessary to love others the way their Father loves them. His love spurs their love to "abound still more and more in real knowledge and all discernment," so they can faithfully do the work that God prepared for them before time began (Philippians 1:9–10; Ephesians 2:8–10).

The apostle Paul, in his Holy Spirit–inspired definition

of *agapē* recorded in 1 Corinthians 13:4–8, describes the characteristics of love that make it so effective in both fueling and cleaning up after the actions of faith:

> Love is patient, love is kind, and is not jealous; love does not brag and is not arrogant, does not act unbecomingly; it does not seek its own, is not provoked, does not take into account a wrong suffered, does not rejoice in unrighteousness, but rejoices with the truth; love bears all things, believes all things, hopes all things, endures all things. Love never fails.

Because *love is patient,* it is "long-tempered" or "long-suffering" with other people.[3] Patient Christians respond to inconsiderate treatment from others without anger or indignation. They selflessly seek the welfare of others. When they must confront sin, they do so gently with the eternal good of the sinner in mind. Of course, God Himself is the ultimate example of "long-suffering" patience (Romans 2:4; 2 Peter 3:9). As we learn about and imitate His perfect patience, we will better obey His commands to love one another.

Because *love is kind,* it is useful, serving, and gracious. Kind Christians are filled with active goodwill. They not only desire the welfare of others, but they actively work to bring it about. They understand that the kindness of God provided them with salvation, and they desire to respond "in kind" by being "kind to one another, tender-hearted, forgiving each other, just as God in Christ also has forgiven you" (Ephesians 4:32).

Because *love is not jealous,* it doesn't begrudge others their success or possessions; nor does it cling tenaciously to what it has been given. Christians who aren't jealous are quick to rejoice with those who rejoice, to weep with those who weep, and to share possessions or the limelight with other people.

Because *love does not brag and is not arrogant,* it does not project a prideful attitude of self-importance. Christians whose faith works in love do not think more highly of themselves than they ought to think (Romans 12:3), and they consider the interests of others more important than their own (Philippians 2:3–4).

Because *love does not act unbecomingly,* it is not characterized by bad manners or rude behavior. Loving Christians are polite, considerate, and sensitive to the needs and feelings of others.

Because *love does not seek its own,* it is not self-focused. Christian love sets its mind on the things above, not on the things of the earth. In doing so, it inspires God's children to ask, "How can I best glorify God and edify others?" Then it stimulates their faith to put revealed knowledge to work— to glorify God and edify others.

Because *love is not provoked and does not take into account a wrong suffered,* it doesn't respond with animosity to personal offenses or harbor resentment against offenders. Although loving Christians may well (in fact, should) be angered by offenses against God and other people, they always seek to respond righteously in those situations.

Because *love does not rejoice in unrighteousness but rejoices with the truth,* it does not take satisfaction in, enjoy, or justify sin. Christians whose faith works in love guard against being entertained by sin, while they refrain from self-righteous boasting about their disciplined restraint. They are righteously offended by the things that offend God, and they do not pass them off lightly or shy away from confronting them. They gently and graciously combat sin and correct errors, because they know that unrepentant sin and compromised truth affects people's souls.

In doing so, they strive not to be "quarrelsome, but . . .

kind to all, able to teach, patient when wronged, with gentleness correcting those who are in opposition," and they pray that "God may grant [sinners and misguided persons] repentance leading to the knowledge of the truth, and they may come to their senses and escape from the snare of the devil, having been held captive by him to do his will" (2 Timothy 2:24–26).

Because *love bears all things, believes all things, hopes all things, endures all things,* it encompass *all things* that are acceptable in God's righteousness. Loving Christians bear with others while protecting them from undue exposure, ridicule, embarrassment, or harm. Even though they are not gullible or undiscerning, neither are they suspicious or cynical. They are trusting by nature and willing to give others the benefit of the doubt. They continue to hope even when their belief in someone's goodness or repentance is stretched to the breaking point, because they know that God's grace often works miracles. And they endure. Christians who love as God first loved them are willing to "remain under" any hardship or trial "for the sake of the chosen."

Love never fails because God is love, and God never fails. Because God loves His children perfectly, their fears are cast out. Because we have come to know and believe that He loves us, we abide in His love and confidently exercise our faith in obedience. The apostle John tells us, "By this we know that we have come to know Him, if we keep His commandments. The one who says, 'I have come to know Him,' and does not keep His commandments, is a liar, and the truth is not in him; but whoever keeps His word, in him the love of God has truly been perfected" (1 John 2:3–5).

Considering all that the love of God accomplishes, it is no exaggeration to say that without God's love working in us, our faith would not move a muscle.

Notes

1. The negation of this word, *astorgos,* meaning "without family affection, unloving, hard-hearted" is used twice in the New Testament, in Romans 1:31 and 2 Timothy 3:3.

2. W. Phillip Keller, *A Layman Looks at the Love of God* (Minneapolis: Bethany House, 1984), 35.

3. Two words are frequently translated as "patient" in the New Testament. The one used in 1 Corinthians 13:4 is *makrothumeō,* which has to do with being patient with people. The other Greek word, *hupomenō,* is translated "endures" in 1 Corinthians 13:7 and has to do with being patient with circumstances or events.

Exercises

Review

1. Describe how love works in our souls analogously to the ways blood works in our bodies.

2. List and briefly define four Greek words that translate into English as "love." Which ones are used in the New Testament? What is significant about this usage?

3. How does the love God gives us when He adopts us into His family help us obey His commandments?

4. List some ways in which faith working in love might produce some debris that needs cleaning up. How does love deal with that debris?

5. List and briefly define each characteristic of love found in 1 Corinthians 13:4–8a. Select five of these characteristics and describe how each one you selected contributes to developing, maintaining, and exercising spiritual strength.

Application

1. Read 1 John 4:7–21 carefully. Based on John's teaching there, describe the role that love plays in developing, maintaining, and exercising spiritual strength. (Hint: Pay particular attention to vv. 16–19.) Think about the relationship between love and spiritual strength described in this passage, and answer the following questions:

   a. Where do you get the love that you need to be spiritually strong?
   b. How does love confirm your standing as a child of God?
   c. How do the Father, the Son, and the Holy Spirit each participate in giving you God's love?
   d. What are your responsibilities toward the love you have been given? Give one or more specific examples of your responsibilities and describe your plan for carrying them out. (Remember to answer the questions Who? What? When? Where? and How?)

2. Identify someone you need spiritual strength to interact with in a way that glorifies God. List one or more reasons why interacting with this person is difficult for you. Then carefully read through the description of love in 1 Corinthians 13:4–8a. Specifically describe how you can apply each characteristic of love listed there in your

relationship with this person. For example: How might you be patient with him or her? In what specific ways can you show kindness to him or her? How might you avoid the appearance of jealousy, bragging, or arrogance? What specific interests of his or hers will you place above your own? After completing this exercise, describe the impact that following through on it will have on your need for strength in dealing with this person. Share your plans for follow-through with someone who loves you enough to encourage you and hold you accountable.

3. Without love, would *your* faith move a muscle? Why or why not? Illustrate your answer with specific examples.

4. Review your memory verses from lessons 1–4, and begin memorizing one or more of the following verses:

   John 13:34–35
   John 14:15
   1 Corinthians 13:4–8a

Digging Deeper

1. Reread carefully this statement by J. I. Packer: "Love framed by truth is the surest verification of the power of God at work in a person." Based upon what you have learned so far in this study, explain this statement thoroughly, paying particular attention to its "key" words and phrases.

6
The Skin of Fellowship

Spiritual unity biblically expressed has always been God's will for His people, and it will always be a blessing to them and a potentially effective witness to those outside the church. —John MacArthur

Most of us overlook the critical role that our skin plays in developing, maintaining, and exercising physical strength. Of all our bodily organs, skin may be the one we most take for granted—until something happens to remind us of how vital it is to our physical health, well-being, and strength. A cut or scrape that becomes infected, a large hole through which blood is pouring, a bad sunburn, or even a ruptured blister will weaken us significantly and jeopardize our ability to function well physically.

Good skin fosters physical strength both directly and indirectly as it provides protection, establishes identity, and projects beauty. Skin fosters physical strength *directly* by defending the internal organs from outside attack. It fosters strength *indirectly* as it maintains our identity and beautifies.

Those of you who have worked in medicine know that one of the greatest dangers associated with full-thickness burns (which destroy all layers of skin) and open fractures (broken bones sticking through the skin) is infection. That's because God created skin with defense mechanisms against deadly germs. The stuff that He put *inside* your body doesn't have those defense mechanisms—for one simple reason. It's supposed to be inside, not outside your skin. When you experience a trauma that causes what's supposed to be on the inside to end up on the outside, infection runs rampant. And you know that infection greatly weakens physical strength. Therefore, good skin is a *protector.*

Skin also provides us with *identity.* If we were all walking around without any skin, we would have a very hard time telling ourselves apart! Skin therefore helps us recognize physical strength in other people. And when we recognize strong people, we can call upon them for help or imitate them in order to grow stronger ourselves.

Skin also displays the beauty of health and strength. Most of us are attracted by physical fitness. We consider physically well-developed, healthy people to be beautiful. They catch our attention and draw us to themselves. Skin plays a role in influencing others.

The spiritual unity of believers expressed in the fellowship of the body of Christ fosters spiritual strength in much the same way that good skin supports physical strength. Scripture reveals that God calls His children into relationships within His family. Those family relationships afford them protection from outside attack while they project a beautiful identity that attracts outsiders and influences others with living truth.

The Skin of Fellowship

One of the reasons our skin functions as it does is that God designed it in layers. The outer layer is called the *epider-*

mis, and the inner layer is called the *dermis.* Since the epidermis interacts with a variety of unpredictable environments, it needs to be strong and resilient. Its partner, the dermis, helps meet this need by supporting and nourishing the epidermis with its rich supply of connective tissue, blood vessels, and nerves. Naturally, the structure and function of the dermis make it the more sensitive of the two layers.

It's fairly easy to draw an analogy between the design of our physical skin and that of our spiritual skin. The fellowship that exists in the body of Christ also consists of two basic layers. An "outer layer" consists of our tough, resilient fellowship with our brothers and sisters in Christ. An "inner layer" forms our highly sensitive, individual and corporate fellowship with God our Father.

Our outer layer of spiritual skin needs to be tough and resilient because it comes in contact with the harsh environment of our fallen world. Strong unity of the Spirit protects us from outside attack while establishing and projecting our beautiful, attractive identity in Christ to those who don't know our God.

Jesus, in His high priestly prayer in John 17, described both the need for and the affect of strong, resilient fellowship among the members of His body. He said we need protection from a world that will hate us because we, like Christ, "are not of the world" even though we have been left in the world as a testimony of God's glory, power, and grace (vv. 14–15). Standing together in unity enables us to withstand the world's hateful onslaught while exhibiting the undeniable reality of our spiritual transformation. Jesus prayed that believers down through the ages

> may all be one; even as Thou, Father, art in Me, and I in Thee, that they also may be in Us; that the world may believe that Thou didst send Me. And the

> glory which Thou hast given Me I have given to them; that they may be one, just as We are one; I in them, and Thou in Me, that they may be perfected in unity, that the world may know that Thou didst send Me, and didst love them, even as Thou didst love Me. (vv. 21–23)

If we are to walk worthy of our high calling in Christ, we need the resilient strength of unified Christian fellowship. However, that strength doesn't grow out of itself. It grows out of our highly sensitive, individual and corporate relationships with God the Father and His Son Jesus Christ through the power of His Holy Spirit. Our "spiritual epidermis" depends upon the nourishment and support of our "spiritual dermis" to maintain its integrity in harsh environments.

Paul told the Ephesians to be "strong *in the Lord,* and in the strength of *His might"* (6:10), and he explained to the Corinthians that *God's power* is perfected in our weakness (2 Corinthians 12:9–10). He knew that the protective, attractive qualities of strong unified fellowship depend upon regular, sensitive communion with God, on both an individual and corporate basis. When fellowship with the Father is interrupted in any way, the fellowship of the body suffers greatly as a result.

Taking Good Care of Our Spiritual Skin

Broken fellowship (just like broken skin) increases our vulnerability to outside attack. It also mars our identity as Christians and blurs the beauty of God that would otherwise shine through our witness. When the skin of a church has been breached, it loses its strength, and that hampers the body's effective fulfillment of God's purposes for it. That's why Scripture admonishes us about the importance of taking good care of our spiritual skin.

We're told to take care of the sensitive inner layer of spiritual skin by "holding fast to the head, from whom the entire body, being supplied and held together by the joints and ligaments, grows with a growth which is from God" (Colossians 2:19). And we are commanded to care for the outer layer of spiritual skin "with all humility and gentleness, with patience, showing forbearance to one another in love, being diligent to preserve the unity of the Spirit in the bond of peace" (Ephesians 4:2–3).

Holding Fast to the Head

Holding fast to the head involves keeping our individual relationships with Jesus Christ in good working order while participating fully in the corporate worship, study, edification, and prayer of the local congregation to which we belong. We must discipline ourselves to make good use of the means of grace God has given us in order to deepen and strengthen our personal and corporate relationships with Him.

The strength of the fellowship depends upon the individual strengths of the "fellowshipers." Therefore each individual Christian must diligently study God's Word (2 Timothy 2:15), confess and repent of sin (1 John 1:9), obey God's commands (Ephesians 4:21–24), and spend time in prayer (Ephesians 6:18). However, we must not lose sight of the fact that the strongest strength is found in numbers. Scripture underscores this great truth by warning us against a "Lone Ranger" approach to Christianity. In Ecclesiastes 4:9–12 we read,

> Two are better than one because they have a good return for their labor. For if either of them falls, the one will lift up his companion. But woe to the one who falls when there is not another to lift him up. Furthermore, if two lie down together, they keep

warm, but how can one be warm alone? And if one can overpower him who is alone, two can resist him. A cord of three strands is not quickly torn apart.

Of course, the stronger each of those "three strands" is, the less likely the cord comprising them will be torn apart.

The writer to the Hebrews picks up on this same theme when he emphasizes the necessity of *corporate* worship, study, edification, and prayer:

> Let us hold fast the confession of our hope without wavering, for He who promised is faithful; and let us consider how to stimulate one another to love and good deeds, not forsaking our own assembling together, as is the habit of some, but encouraging one another; and all the more, as you see the day drawing near (10:23–25).

Corporate worship and study under the Spirit-led leadership of God-ordained pastors and teachers equips us to "hold fast the confession of our hope without wavering." And joint edification and prayer stimulates and encourages all of God's children to pursue faithful, obedient service. We don't get that by operating in isolation.

Working hard at maintaining our individual and corporate sensitivity to God's voice by submitting ourselves to His ordained means of grace will keep our spiritual dermis healthy and strong. But we must also take care of our outer layer of spiritual skin. Cracks and tears in that layer inevitably harm the inner layer as well, and thus weaken the ability of the body of Christ to function.

Preserving the Unity of the Spirit

Preserving the unity of the Spirit in the bond of peace is one of the Christian's best protective devices, as well as being a powerful witnessing tool. When we *stand together* in the midst of our fallen, hostile environment, we draw strength from each other, unite our abilities in common effort, and shine brighter than we could ever hope to alone. Paul reminded the embattled Philippians of the importance of taking good care of their spiritual epidermis when he wrote, "If therefore there is any encouragement in Christ, if there is any consolation of love, if there is any fellowship of the Spirit, if any affection and compassion, make my joy complete by being of the same mind, maintaining the same love, united in spirit, intent on one purpose" (2:1–2).

Then he went on to explain, quite specifically, *how* they could develop and maintain critical strength and resilience in the body of Christ's epidermis by living out three basic attitudes in their relationships with each other. The primary attitude they must express to each other is that of *humility*:

> Do nothing from selfishness or empty conceit, but with humility of mind let each of you regard one another as more important than himself; do not merely look out for your own personal interests, but also for the interests of others. Have this attitude in yourselves which was also in Christ Jesus, who, although He existed in the form of God, did not regard equality with God a thing to be grasped, but emptied Himself, taking the form of a bond-servant, and being made in the likeness of men (vv. 3–7).

We show affection, compassion, and mutual love when we look out for the interests of others with as much fervor as—or *more* fervor than—we look out for our own. Unbreakable bonds are forged in the fire of self-sacrificial service to our brothers and sisters in Christ. Such dedicated regard for others flies to their aid when they need protection, and attractively displays God's love, mercy, and grace before a lost world.

The second attitude that will insure the health of our outer layer of spiritual skin is *submission*. Paul describes it like this:

> So then, my beloved, just as you have always obeyed, not as in my presence only, but now much more in my absence, work out your salvation with fear and trembling; for it is God who is at work in you, both to will and to work for His good pleasure (vv. 12–13).

Fellowship of the Spirit expressed in intense like-mindedness and a singular purpose builds on submissive obedience to God rather than emotion. Frankly, I don't always "feel like" working out my salvation by doing what God commands me to do in His Word. And I'm sure you don't either. That is particularly true for me (and I'm sure for you too) when those commands involve looking out for the interests of people I do not like, or who dislike me. I tend to bristle at the very idea of considering them more important than myself. But, if I live out my emotions, instead of obeying my Father, I will weaken the church body's outer layer of skin. That will result in weakening our defenses and lessening our impact on a dark, needy world. Is it worth it? No, it is not.

The third attitude Paul advised the Philippians to live out in their relationships with each other is *contentment*. He puts it bluntly: "Do all things without grumbling or disputing" (v. 14). Alternate translations read, "Do all things without complaining and disputing" (NKJV); ". . . without grumbling and arguing" (NKJV margin); "Do everything without complaining or arguing" (NIV).

Paul doesn't give us any outs. He doesn't say, "Do *most things* without grumbling, disputing, complaining or arguing." And he doesn't say, "Do all things without grumbling, disputing, complaining, or arguing—except when you are dealing with self-righteous sinners, hardened pagans, the Motor Vehicle Department, or the federal bureaucracy."

Do you find Paul's blunt words as hard to obey as I do? If you do, it is most likely because you struggle as much I do with being *content* in all situations of life. Perhaps one of the most difficult of our "contentment challenges" is living in unity with the particular people God chose to place in our families, our neighborhoods, our schools, and our churches. It would be so much easier to live in contentment with better people! Ah, but of course, they are saying the very same thing about you and me.

Strong, resilient fellowship demands an attitude of contentment in our relationships with sinful people. Developing and maintaining that attitude of contentment requires us to work hard at compassion, kindness, humility, gentleness, patience, and forgiveness (see Colossians 3:12–13). That is hard work, but it's certainly worth it.

What happens when Christians take good care of their spiritual epidermis by living out attitudes of humility, submission, and contentment? Paul says that we will prove ourselves "to be blameless and innocent, children of God above reproach in the midst of a crooked and perverse generation, among whom you appear as lights in the world, holding fast the word of life" (Philippians 2:14–16). In other words, we will be strong and courageous, defending one another from harm and projecting an attractive identity to those in the world who don't know our God. We'll have good spiritual skin.

The Components of Strength

We have completed our overview of the *components* of spiritual strength—the raw materials we need to be strong in the Lord. Do you remember what they are? The life of salvation, the good bones of knowledge, the muscles of faith, the blood of love, and the skin of fellowship. Do you remember that we emphasized in our discussions that our Father God gives us all of these essential components of strength when He adopts us into His family? And that we also indicated that simply having them in our possession would not make us strong?

Well, now that we know what we have to work with, it's time to start "working out" with what we have. The next four lessons will help us develop and implement a spiritual workout routine under the watchful eye of our Personal Spiritual Trainer. In lesson 7, we'll look at the ways that He helps us work out our salvation. Then in lessons 8–10, we'll study the three essential elements of a spiritual workout routine: the good diet of Scripture, the diligent exercise of obedience, and the rejuvenating rest found in prayer.

Exercises

Review

1. Describe the role your skin plays in developing, maintaining, and exercising physical strength. Relate this to the role spiritual unity in the fellowship of the body of Christ plays in developing, maintaining, and exercising spiritual strength.

2. How does the design of your physical skin contribute to its bodily function? Explain the analogy between the design of your physical skin and the design of your spiritual skin.

3. Read all of John 17. In that chapter, how did Jesus describe the need for and affect of strong, resilient fel-

lowship among the members of His body? How is this fellowship among believers nourished and supported?

4. Why is taking care of our spiritual skin important to our spiritual health? What "directions for care" do we find in Ephesians 4:2–3 and Colossians 2:19?

5. Describe our need to participate in both individual and corporate fellowship with God. What are some ways we can enter into fellowship with God both individually and corporately?

6. How does Paul describe the "ways and means" of maintaining the unity of the Spirit in the bond of peace in Philippians 2:1–16?

7. List and briefly describe each of the components of spiritual strength we have studied so far. Then list the three essential elements of a spiritual workout routine.

Application

1. How well are you taking care of your spiritual skin? Answer that question carefully by thinking about the following:

   a. *Taking good care of your spiritual dermis:* How well do you make use of individual and corporate means of grace? Do you read your Bible daily? How often do you read it completely? Do you study the Bible individually and with other believers? Do you have an established time devoted to individual prayer? Do you maintain an attitude of prayer throughout your day? How often do you meet with other believers for prayer? How sensitive are you to the Holy Spirit's conviction of sin in your life? When was the last time you were convicted about a specific sin? What did you do about it? Do you meet regularly for worship with other believers? Do you worship God on your own? Do you have one or two close Christian friends with whom you can discuss deep, sensitive issues?

b. *Taking good care of your spiritual epidermis:* How tough and resilient is your fellowship with other believers? List several specific examples of ways in which you have considered the interests of others more important than your own during the past week. When was the last time you gave up something you really wanted so someone else could have something he or she really needed? How have you expressed love and consideration to a believer you don't like or to one who doesn't like you? Are you content with the family, neighborhood, school, and/or church in which God has placed you? Do you relate to the people around you with kindness, patience, gentleness, compassion, and forgiveness? Give specific examples. Select ten people at random from your church directory: Do you know where they work, or where they go to school? What do you know about their extended families? In what ministries are they involved? What difficulties are they facing right now? How can you help them stand firm against attacks from the world, the flesh, and the Devil?

Based upon your consideration of these questions, how effectively do you believe your spiritual skin is functioning as a protector? How well does it project identity and beauty to those who don't know God? What steps can you take to improve its functioning in those areas?

When will you begin taking these steps? Who loves you enough to encourage you and hold you accountable for following through with your plan?

2. Read Donald S. Whitney's book, *Spiritual Disciplines for the Christian Life,* and pick three areas of spiritual discipline that need work in your life. Make and describe a detailed plan for implementing Dr. Whitney's suggestions in your daily life in each of these areas. Can you think of other ways in which you can strengthen your exercise of these particular disciplines? If so, describe them. Who will you ask to hold you accountable for following through on your plan?

3. Review your memory verses from previous lessons. Then begin memorizing one or more of the following:

   Ecclesiastes 4:9–12
   Ephesians 4:1–3
   Philippians 2:1–2

Digging Deeper

1. Ponder the idea presented in this lesson that our outer layer of spiritual skin (fellowship with our brothers and sisters in Christ) must be tough and resilient, whereas our inner layer of spiritual skin (individual and corporate fellowship with God) must be highly sensitive. Consider the following questions while you are pondering: What is tough, resilient fellowship? What characteristics of *believers* give rise to the need for tough, resilient fellowship among them? What characteristics of *our world* give rise to the need for tough, resilient fellowship among believers? Is tough, resilient fellowship also insensitive? How might tough, resilient fellowship

demonstrate great sensitivity toward others? In what ways does the sensitivity we express toward one another differ from our sensitivity to God? How do individual and corporate fellowship complement each other? How do they support our tough, resilient fellowship with one another? When you have finished pondering these things, write a brief explanation of the relationship between your two layers of spiritual skin.

PART 3

The Spiritual Workout Routine

7

Our Personal
Spiritual Trainer

*Reality reminds us that all the will in the world may not
make us what we want to become. When it comes to will
power, will is common but power is rare.*

—Os Guinness

On days when my husband comes home for lunch, we
frequently listen to Rush Limbaugh's radio program while
we eat. Whether we agree with him or not, he usually
gives us food for thought while we enjoy food for our stomachs. One day last summer, Rush devoted part of the program to answering a question he hears again and again
from his fans: "How did you manage to lose so much
weight?"

He explained that he had known, for many years, *how*
to lose weight. He knew it required eating a well-balanced,
nutritious diet while getting enough exercise and adequate
rest. However, his hectic schedule and preoccupation with
work kept him from putting what he knew into practice.
Although he understood the benefits of being physically fit,

he wasn't willing to divert from his other activities the time required to achieve it.

However, soon after his marriage, "getting in shape" became a priority. But since he and his new bride both had hectic schedules and were preoccupied with their work, he realized that he needed some outside help. So he hired an expert to plan and cook meals, and to work a reasonable exercise and rest regimen into his schedule. Rush Limbaugh frankly admitted that he had "shaped up" because he had the money to pay for the expertise that he needed. And if you've seen "before" and "after" pictures of him, you know that he got his money's worth out of the arrangement!

I'm sure most of us, at one time or another, have thought about beginning a workout routine to lose weight, build our physical strength, or simply improve our overall health and vitality. If you are one of those people, you obviously see benefit in being physically fit. You may even know *how* to become physically fit—eat right, exercise well, and get adequate rest. However, your life is almost as busy as Limbaugh's, and you don't have his money. So you're still carrying around those ten extra pounds, and you still can't get the lid off that jar of dill pickles, and you still run out of energy 'long about noon.

If you are like most of us who would like to be physically fit, you may have learned through sad experience that *knowing how* to achieve physical fitness won't bring it about. You have to *work* at it. You have to determine which foods to include in your diet; and then you have to devote time to buying and preparing them. You have to learn which forms of exercise are appropriate for your age and lifestyle; and then you have to expend effort performing them. You have to find out how much rest is sufficient for you; and then you have to organize your activities to make sure that you get it. Perhaps that is why so few people are physically fit. Physical fitness requires more thought and effort than we want to spare. And most folks can't afford to hire expert help.

Well, spiritual fitness isn't much different. I have yet to meet a committed Christian who doesn't want to be spiritually fit. Those of us who are devoted to Christ see the great benefits of spiritual fitness. Interestingly, many of us also know how to become spiritually fit. Some of us even teach other Christians how to go about it. But when we look around our fallen world, we simply don't see many spiritually fit Christians.

Why is that? Well, we are so very busy, and spiritual fitness takes so much time. Our energy resources are stretched to the limit already, and spiritual fitness takes so much effort. Our knowledge of Scripture is so academic, and spiritual fitness requires practical application. We want to be spiritually fit, but we just don't have the power to make it happen. As Os Guinness put it, "When it comes to will power, will is common but power is rare."[1]

We need help to become spiritually fit—powerful help. And the good news is that we don't have to buy it! The powerful help that we need isn't for sale at any price. That powerful help is a Person, God's Holy Spirit, who is given by Jesus Christ to each one of us at the moment we are adopted into God's family.

Our Personal Spiritual Trainer

Each one of us has, living within him or her, the world's greatest expert on spiritual fitness. This expert knows all there is to know about a good diet of Scripture, the diligent exercise of obedience, and the rejuvenating rest of God-centered prayer. He is ready, willing, and able to guide our every step as we work out with these essential ingredients of spiritual fitness. In keeping with our analogy, let's think of Him as our Personal Spiritual Trainer. However, His presence alone won't make us strong. If we want to be strong, we have to work hard at submitting to His authority and doing what He tells us.

Paul described our responsibility to make wise use of the Spirit's invaluable services when he told the Philippians to work out their salvation with fear and trembling because God, in the Person of His indwelling Spirit, was at work in them both to will and to work for His good pleasure (2:12–13). You may remember from a previous lesson that God declared through Isaiah the prophet that He would accomplish all His good pleasure (46:9–10). And He uses Paul's words to the Philippians to assure us that one of the ways He works out His good pleasure is through the work of His Holy Spirit in the lives of His children.

The great Puritan teacher John Owen described the work of the Holy Spirit in terms of counteracting or overcoming the "natural futility of the mind in its depraved condition found among believers."[2] The natural futility of our depraved minds weakens us spiritually in three ways, according to Owen.

> Firstly, it makes the believer waver and be unstable and fickle in the holy duties of meditation, prayer and hearing the word. The mind wanders and is distracted by many worldly thoughts. Secondly, this instability is the cause of backsliding in believers, leading them to conform to the world and its habits and customs which are vain and foolish. And thirdly, this futility of the mind deceives believers into providing for the flesh and the lusts of the flesh. It can and often does lead to self-indulgence."[3]

Inattention to duty, unstable backsliding, and foolish self-indulgence—they are a troublesome trio that spawns spiritual weakness, not strength. But our depraved minds are naturally attracted by its Siren's Song. Resisting its call requires heeding the voice of God's indwelling Spirit instead. He calls us to turn from our worldly preoccupations and to set our minds on the things above where Christ is seated at the right hand of God.

The Holy Spirit works in us by exalting Christ in our sight. On the night before Jesus died, He described for His disciples the *modus operandi* of our Personal Spiritual Trainer:

> When the Helper comes, whom I will send to you from the Father, that is the Spirit of truth, who proceeds from the Father, He will bear witness of Me. . . . He shall glorify Me; for He shall take of Mine, and shall disclose it to you. All things that the Father has are Mine; therefore I said, that He takes of Mine, and will disclose it to you. (John 15:26; 16:14–15)

Jesus told His disciples that the Holy Spirit works in the lives of believers by focusing their attention on the things of Christ. Therefore when we submit to His guidance, we set our minds on Christ and direct our efforts toward conforming ourselves to His image. The more like Him we become, the more spiritually fit we will be. The more spiritually fit we become, the more spiritual strength we will have. And the more spiritually strong we become, the better equipped we will be to walk worthy of our high calling of glorifying God and enjoying Him forever.

We could say that the Holy Spirit's "job description" includes indwelling believers for the purpose of directing their hearts and minds toward the pursuit of Christlikeness. That's a big job, given our natural depraved inclinations. But our Personal Spiritual Trainer can handle it. All He requires from us is willing submission to His direction.

Working out our salvation under His expert guidance guarantees successful achievement of spiritual fitness.

Our Personal Spiritual Trainer assists us in our spiritual workout routine as He enlightens our minds to absorb the truths of the Bible, empowers us to obey its commands, and provides much-needed rest through God-centered prayer.

The Spirit Enlightens Our Minds

The Holy Spirit helps us absorb the truths of the Bible by guiding our minds as we interact with God's truth. He helps us think well, and He blesses us with understanding as we read and study the Bible. Paul describes His critical work of illumining Scripture in 1 Corinthians 2:10–16.

> For to us God revealed [His great truths] through the Spirit; for the Spirit searches all things, even the depths of God. For who among men knows the thoughts of a man except the spirit of the man, which is in him? Even so the thoughts of God no one knows except the Spirit of God.
>
> Now we have received, not the spirit of the world, but the Spirit who is from God, that we might know the things freely given to us by God, which things we also speak, not in words taught by human wisdom, but in those taught by the Spirit, combining spiritual thoughts with spiritual words.
>
> But a natural man does not accept the things of the Spirit of God; for they are foolishness to him, and he cannot understand them, because they are spiritually appraised. But he who is spiritual appraises all things, yet he himself is appraised by no man. For who has known the mind of the Lord, that he should instruct Him? But we have the mind of Christ.

Whenever I read that passage, I am amazed by God's love and grace. Not only has He *revealed* His truth to us in Scripture through the Spirit's work of inspiring the writers—but He sends that same Spirit to live in us and guide our *understanding* of the truths that we read. God knows that our minds are inclined toward futility and are consequently unable to comprehend rightly the revelation of Scripture. And His compassion and love toward His children spurred Him to take action to meet our need for practical understanding.

The first time I tried to use the weight machines at the gym at the University of New Mexico, I was completely baffled. Those machines had been designed by very smart people who knew a lot about physical fitness, and each one came equipped with well-written instructions. But my lack of weight-training experience interfered with my practical understanding. I needed an expert to help me comprehend those instructions. And just such an expert jumped to my aid.

My observant, concerned teacher, a skilled weight-trainer, saw my difficulty and patiently took time to explain those instructions. In much the same way, God sends His Spirit with His children into His Word. He knows that our lack of spiritual experience leaves us in need of expert help, which He graciously provides.

The Spirit Helps Us Obey

I found it interesting that my weight-training teacher at UNM did not walk away as soon as I understood the written instructions. He stayed and helped me *put into practice* what I had learned. God's Holy Spirit does the same thing. His expert assistance doesn't stop with illumining our understanding of Scripture; He also helps us apply what we know.

James tells us not to be "merely hearers" of truth, but to prove ourselves "doers of the word" (1:22). Since fallen depraved sinners (that's you and I) lack any "natural ability" to obey God's commands, grow in Christlikeness, and gain spiritual strength, we must depend on the Spirit for the power we need.

Paul encouraged the Corinthians to rely *on the Spirit* as they obediently carried out their work in ministry. First, he reminded them that they were not adequate in themselves for the task, but that their adequacy came from God through the work of the Spirit (2 Corinthians 3:5–6). Then he assured them that the work of the Spirit could not fail to produce glorious results (vv. 7–11), and he affirmed that their bold hope was well grounded in this assurance (vv. 12–16). Finally, he fired up their commitment to faithful obedience by declaring that the Spirit's presence within them gave them "liberty" to obey God's commands, and that this work of God's Spirit was actively transforming them into the image of Christ (vv. 17–18).

J. I. Packer summed up this help we receive from our Personal Spiritual Trainer:

> His blessing on the Bible we read, and on the Christian instruction we receive, persuades us of the truth of Christianity. He shows us how God's promises and demands bear on our lives. His new-creation action at the center of our personal being so changes and energizes us that we do in fact obey the truth. The persuasion at the conscious level is powerful. The heart-changing action that produces Christian commitment is almighty. . . . It is the Spirit's power that generates all the goodness of the Christian's good works."[4]

The Spirit Provides Rest in God-Centered Prayer

I also found it quite interesting that my weight-training teacher at UNM warned his eager students *against* working out on the machines every day of the week. "Your body needs rest," he told us, "if it's going to be strong."

And of course, if our souls are to be strong, they need rest too. Much of the spiritual rest that we need comes to us in prayer, and God's Holy Spirit is our Helper there also. Paul told the Romans that the Spirit helps our weakness, "for we do not know how to pray as we should, but the Spirit Himself intercedes for us with groanings too deep for words; and He who searches the hearts knows what the mind of the Spirit is, because He intercedes for the saints according to the will of God" (8:26–27).

In our next three lessons, we will look in detail at the essential ingredients of a spiritual strength-building workout routine: the good diet of Scripture, the diligent exercise of obedience, and the rejuvenating rest found in prayer. As we work through those lessons, our Personal Spiritual Trainer will be at work helping us to understand, to obey, and to rest. And He will do His work by turning our attention toward the things of Christ.

Because God's Spirit works the way that He does, it's easy for us to forget that He is here. He works almost invisibly, exalting Christ, not Himself. That is why we devoted an entire lesson to the Spirit's indispensable role in our spiritual workout routine. We need this reminder not to neglect and ignore Him, but to acknowledge with gratitude His empowering presence. *Thank you, Lord God, for the gift of Your Spirit.*

Notes

1. Os Guinness, *The Call: Finding and Fulfilling the Central Purpose of Your Life* (Nashville: Word, 1998), 23.

2. John Owen, *The Holy Spirit: The Treasures of John Owen for Today's Readers,* abridged and made easy to read by R. J. K. Law (Carlisle, Pa.: Banner of Truth, 1998), 58.

3. Ibid.

4. J. I. Packer, *Rediscovering Holiness* (Ann Arbor, Mich.: Servant, 1992), 226–27.

Exercises

Review

1. Relate the difficulties of getting and staying physically fit with the difficulties most Christians have getting and staying spiritually fit.

2. Read Isaiah 46:8–11 and Philippians 2:12–13. Note carefully what each passage teaches about God's "good pleasure." Then read 2 Corinthians 3:1–18 and explain the indwelling Holy Spirit's role in bringing about God's good pleasure.

3. How did John Owen describe the work of the Holy Spirit in believers? Why is this work necessary? How does He accomplish it? (See John 15:26; 16:14–15.) What does He require from us?

4. Read 1 Corinthians 2:10–16 and express in your own words how the Holy Spirit helps us understand Scripture.

5. Read 2 Corinthians 3:5–18 and James 1:22–25. Then express in your own words how the Holy Spirit helps us obey God's commands.

6. Read Romans 8:27–28 and express in your own words how the Holy Spirit helps us pray.

Application

1. Have you ever thought about starting a physical workout routine? If so, did you follow through on your plan? If you did, explain what helped you devote the time and effort necessary to get and stay physically fit. If you did not, explain what hindered you most. Did you learn anything from your success or failure with a physical workout routine that may help you implement a spiritual workout routine? If so, explain.

2. Make a list of all the spiritual workout activities in which you are currently involved. List these under the three headings of "Good Diet of Scripture," "Strenuous Exercise of Obedience," and "Rejuvenating Rest of Prayer." Draw a double line under your current activities. Then list other activities you believe you should add to your list. Make a plan to begin implementing one or more of these activities this week. Refer to this list and adjust it as we work through the next three lessons.

3. Review your memory verses from lessons 1–6 (no new verses for this lesson).

Digging Deeper

1. Develop a "lesson plan" or "teaching outline" emphasizing several specific ways in which inattention to duty, backsliding, and foolish self-indulgence contribute to spiritual weakness. Then develop a follow-up lesson plan or teaching outline emphasizing how submission to the guidance of the Holy Spirit will counteract these tendencies of our depraved minds and build spiritual strength. Use your lesson plan or teaching outline in a Sunday school class, in a Bible study, in a discipling relationship, or with your children.

8

The Good Diet
of Scripture

Our love for the Word is the pulse of our spiritual health.
— J. C. Ryle

The great Anglican bishop J. C. Ryle is one of my favorite authors. Not only is his work solidly God-centered and focused on the things above, but his way with words helps me remember the great truths he taught. The quotation above is a case in point. Its concise, memorable clarity adds an important dimension to the analogy we're using to study spiritual strength.

In lesson 5, we equated spiritual love (*agapē*) with physical blood and compared the work of the blood in the body to the work of love in the soul. You know, of course, that blood rushing through veins creates a pulse. You also know that pulse rates reveal much more than the mere presence of blood in a body. They also indicate quite a bit about a person's overall health, fitness, and emotional state.

Interestingly, our love for the Word reveals those same kinds of things about our spiritual condition. A strong, regular love for God's Word characterizes people who are spiritually healthy and fit, as it does people who possess a serene quiet spirit despite their circumstances. That's why a good friend of mine is fond of saying that a Bible that's falling apart usually belongs to a person who isn't. Love for God's Word motivates us to feast upon its essential spiritual nutrients.

Naturally, people who love nutritious food tend to be physically healthy and strong. In much the same way, Christians who love God's Word tend to be spiritually healthy and strong. Their love of Scripture motivates them to digest its truths well.

Each component of physical strength that we have discussed (life, bones, muscles, blood, and skin) requires a consistent, balanced intake of physical nutrients to function effectively. Each atrophies quickly when improperly nourished. Similarly, the corresponding components of spiritual strength (salvation, knowledge, faith, love, and fellowship) depend just as heavily for their effective functioning upon a consistent, balanced intake of Scripture.

It's important to emphasize that adequate physical and spiritual nourishment must be both *consistent* and *balanced*. When I studied nutrition in college, I learned that very few of the essential physical nutrients can be stored by the body for later use. Most nutrients, if not used within a certain period of time, are either eliminated from the body, or restructured and stored as fat (usually on our hips!).

No reasonable person expects to eat once a month or even once a week and remain healthy and strong. And most reasonable people (excluding those who get hooked on fad diets) understand that eating all protein, or all carbohydrates, or all fats will not foster health and strength either. A strong, healthy body depends upon consistent, balanced nourishment.

We will see, as we work through this lesson, that a strong healthy soul demands the same kind of input. Just as with physical nourishment, we need spiritual nourishment every day of our lives. Most of us have a little stored physical fat that will sustain us for a few days of fasting, but unfortunately very few of us have any spiritual fat at all on our bones. If we want to be strong in God's service, we must be in His Word daily—usually several times daily!

Spiritual fitness simply cannot be maintained on one sermon a week or on those Vacation Bible School memory verses we learned as kids. Neither will it thrive on an imbalanced intake. D. L. Moody said it well: "A man can no more take in a supply of grace for the future than he can eat enough for the next six months. . . . We must draw upon God's boundless store of grace from day to day as we need it."[1] Spiritual health and strength depend upon a consistent, balanced diet of Scripture.

If I Were the Devil . . .

Another of my favorite authors is J. I. Packer. His work is also solidly God-centered and focused on things above. And although he is not as consistently eloquent as J. C. Ryle, every so often he comes up with a truly unforgettable gem. Take a look at this sparkling jewel from the introduction to R. C. Sproul's, *Knowing Scripture:*

> If I were the devil, one of my first aims would be to stop folk from digging into the Bible. Knowing that it is the Word of God, teaching men to know and love and serve the God of the Word, I should do all I could to surround it with the spiritual equivalent of pits, thorn hedges, and man traps, to frighten people off. . . . How? Well, I should try to distract all clergy from preaching and teaching the Bible, and

spread the feeling that to study this ancient book directly is a burdensome extra which modern Christians can forgo without loss. I should broadcast doubts about the truth and relevance and good sense and straightforwardness of the Bible, and if any still insisted on reading it, I should lure them into assuming that the benefit of the practice lies in the noble and tranquil feelings evoked by it rather than in noting what Scripture actually says. At all costs I should want to keep them from using their minds in a disciplined way to get the measure of its message.[2]

The Devil knows that the best way to weaken Christians is through malnutrition. If he can keep us away from the nutrition of Scripture, he can also keep us weak and ineffective in our service to God.

Paul warns us against falling for the Devil's devices. In Colossians 3:16, he commands us to let the Word dwell in us richly. The Word "dwell" paints a picture of settling down and being at home. In other words, Scripture should not be considered a "special guest" in our lives, but a functioning part of life itself. When Scripture settles down and is at home in our lives, it does not come and go on special occasions. Rather, it is thoroughly integrated into every routine activity.

If you have ever moved into a new house or apartment, you know that "settling down and being at home" take a lot of hard work. So it shouldn't surprise you that letting the Word of Christ richly dwell within you requires hard work also. Before the revealed truth of God will settle down and be at home in your life, you have to get it off the page and into your system. And, of course, the best way to do that is with a consistent, balanced diet of Scripture.

A good physical diet supports the body's functions by balancing a consistent intake of food with the right amounts of protein, carbohydrates, fats, vitamins, minerals, and water. Likewise, a good spiritual diet supports the soul's functions by balancing its intake of Scripture with the right amounts of listening, reading, studying, memorizing, and meditating.[3] Just as all the physical nutrients are needed to work together to keep us physically fit, all of the spiritual activities associated with scriptural intake must work together to keep us spiritually strong. We cannot leave one or two out of the mix and expect to maintain our spiritual health.

Listening to the Word

Jesus emphasized the importance of listening to God's Word when He said, "Blessed are those who hear the word of God, and observe it" (Luke 11:28). Psalm 138:2 tells us that God has magnified His Word according to (or together with) His name. Since God exalts His Word to such a high level, we know that hearing, understanding, and responding to it is very important. In fact, it is so important that God calls and specifically equips pastors and teachers to expound it for us. In Nehemiah 8:6–8, we read,

> Then Ezra blessed the LORD the great God. And all the people answered, "Amen, Amen!" while lifting up their hands; then they bowed low and worshiped the LORD with their faces to the ground. Also Jeshua, Bani, Sherebiah, Jamin, Akkub, Shabbethai, Hodiah, Maaseiah, Kelita, Azariah, Jozabad, Hanan, Pelaiah, and the Levites, explained the law to the people while the people remained in their place. And they read from the book, from the law of God, translating [or explaining] to give the sense so that they understood the reading.

Paul told the Ephesians that God "gave some as apostles, and some as prophets, and some as evangelists, and some as pastors and teachers, for the equipping of the saints for the work of service, to the building up of the body of Christ" (4:11–12). And he admonished Timothy, one of those pastors, to "give attention to the public reading of Scripture, to exhortation and teaching" (1 Timothy 4:13); and to "preach the word; be ready in season and out of season; reprove, rebuke, exhort, with great patience and instruction" (2 Timothy 4:2).

Listening to God's Word so as to understand and apply it requires discipline on our parts—largely because our fallen natures are so easily distracted by the things of the world. Listening well to God's Word requires focused concentration, but our culture's addiction to hustle, bustle, and noise consistently draws our attention away from devotion to Scripture.

Many centuries ago, the prophet Amos predicted a coming famine "for hearing the words of the LORD" (8:11). And I think it's here. It's not that the words of the Lord have ceased being expounded. We are blessed in our day with an abundance of excellent preaching and teaching—in pulpits and classrooms, as well as on audio and video tape, radio, and TV. The problem is *not* a lack of good preaching and teaching. Amos said the famine would be one of *hearing.* The truth is being proclaimed, but we are not listening.

Jeremiah Burroughs, in his 1648 treatise *Gospel Worship,* advises Christians to sharpen their listening skills by actively preparing themselves to hear the Word preached and taught. "There must first be preparation," he said. "When you come to hear the Word, if you would sanctify God's name, you must possess your souls with what it is you are going to hear."[4] That was good advice in 1648, and it is even better advice today.

Reading the Word

Getting the scriptural nourishment we need to be strong in God's service also requires us to learn how to read well. Now if you're thinking, *Wait a minute—I know how to read,* let me assure you that I'm not referring to simply recognizing words on a page. Reading well generates comprehension of what we have read. And that involves absorbing the concepts described by the words on the page.

We live in a visually oriented culture that is systematically destroying our desire and ability to read well for any purpose other than entertainment. Neil Postman, in his book *Amusing Ourselves to Death,* explains how this has happened. He demonstrates that certain forms of communication lend themselves to transmitting certain types of information. Smoke signals, for instance, cannot adequately convey profound philosophical ideas. The printed page, on the other hand, is uniquely suited to transmitting deep meaningful concepts, like those found in Scripture. As we have become more oriented toward the visual world of television and movies, our desire for and ability to absorb information has grown more superficial. Our loss of appetite for the printed page has resulted in a loss of capacity to think deeply and well.

Therefore, digesting the truths of the Bible requires us to recover a taste for print. The profound truths of Scripture simply cannot be transmitted adequately through visual images. We will never get as much out of the movie as we will from the Book. But reading the Book takes some serious chewing. We must apply ourselves if we want to read Scripture well.

We must, first of all, set aside regular periods of time (15 minutes a day is a good start) when we can and will read intently without distraction. Second, we should read according to a well-thought-out plan that focuses on covering the entire Bible within a set time frame. Most such plans allow us to read the Bible in a year or less. Reading the whole Book on a regular basis is essential to understanding its overall message. Most Christians read Scripture topically, much as they would an encyclopedia. They read certain portions when they are interested in certain bits of information. And they derive a great deal of benefit from what they learn. But there is a danger in reading the Bible in that way exclusively.

The Bible was not written as a handy reference manual. Rather, it tells a story—the story of God's display of His glory in the salvation of sinners. Rightly understanding and applying *segments* of Scripture requires us to see them within the context of Scripture's overall message. I am convinced that most of the truth-abuse we see in the church today results from our failure to read the Bible from cover to cover to get the gist of its story. The key to understanding the Bible is context, context, context. And we get that from reading, reading, reading—reading regularly, reading intently, and reading completely.

Studying Scripture

Studying Scripture is an extension of that kind of reading. Studying the Bible begins with a conscious commitment to read *observantly* for the purpose of determining precisely what Scripture is saying. Observant reading includes paying attention to immediate and broader contexts, key words, grammatical constructions, tone of "voice," audience, and literary genres. Disciplining ourselves to read observantly helps us resist the temptation to force the passage to say what we want it to say, or what we expect it to say, or what we think it should say, instead of what it actually says.

Studying the Bible also involves interpreting what the Bible means by what it says. Many Christians who lack formal theological training do not believe they can do this, but the truth is, they can. In fact, if they want to be strong in God's service, they must. Sitting back and accepting someone else's interpretation of Scripture is both enervating and dangerous. Luke commended the noble-minded Bereans for eagerly listening to Paul and then "examining the Scriptures daily, to see whether these things were so" (Acts 17:11). If *they* rightly examined Paul's teaching in the light of biblical interpretation, we should also be examining what we are taught today.

Interpreting the majority of the Bible's message is not necessarily difficult, but it does require humble submission to the Holy Spirit (see 1 Corinthians 2:6–16) and basic training in a few study skills. If you haven't yet learned these basic skills, there are a number of good training manuals available, one of which is included in the Light for Your Path Series.[5]

Of course, studying Scripture is never complete until we apply what we have learned. James says that if we understand God's truth but fail to practice it, we delude ourselves; however, when we become effectual doers of what we have learned, we will be blessed (James 1:22–25).

The great blessings that result from the study of Scripture are available to all believers in Jesus Christ, but tragically, very few ever receive them. That's because most Christians these days do not study Scripture. And the primary reason they don't is distressingly simple: study takes time and effort. R. C. Sproul sums it up well: "Here then, is the real problem of our negligence. We fail in our duty to study God's Word not so much because it is difficult to understand, not so much because it is dull and boring, but because it is work. Our problem is not a lack of intelligence or a lack of passion. Our problem is that we are lazy."[6]

As we've said before, merely having the good bones of

knowledge in our possession won't make us strong in God's service. We have to work out with what we've been given.

Memorizing and Meditating on Scripture

You are probably aware that good food must be well digested before it will benefit our physical bodies. As food passes from our mouths into our stomachs and through our intestines, its vital nutrients are extracted, broken down, rearranged chemically, and absorbed into our systems. Digestion begins in our mouths as we chew, and it continues in our stomachs as busy enzymes start working. However, the bulk of digestion occurs while that food makes its way slowly through yards and yards of intestines. It is here that most of the vital nutrients are removed and transported to those eagerly waiting bodily systems.

In much the same way, the truths of the Bible must be well digested before our souls will benefit from them. Digesting Scripture begins as we hear and read it, and continues as we devote time and effort to diligent study. But the real work of digesting its vital nutrients takes place as God's Word slowly absorbs into our systems during long hours devoted to memorization and meditation.

Memorizing Scripture stores up vital nutrients for quick, ready access whenever they're needed, and meditation keeps them circulating through our hearts and minds. Only when the truths we are hearing, reading, and studying are digested well through memorization and meditation will we consistently set our minds on God and His purposes. Saturating our souls with the nutrition of Scripture is what keeps us "seeking the things above, where Christ is, seated at the right hand of God" (Colossians 3:1).

Maurice Roberts captured the importance of thoroughly digesting Scripture when he said,

Our age has been sadly deficient in what may be termed spiritual greatness. At the root of this is the modern disease of shallowness. We are all too impatient to meditate on the faith we profess. . . . It is not the busy skimming over religious books or the careless hastening through religious duties which makes for a strong Christian faith. Rather, it is the unhurried meditation on gospel truths and the exposing of our minds to these truths that yields the fruit of sanctified character.[7]

We who desire to be strong in God's service should hear and heed his insightful words.

Notes

1. Quoted in John Blanchard, *How to Enjoy Your Bible* (Colchester, England: Evangelical Press, 1984), 104.

2. J. I. Packer, foreword to R. C. Sproul, *Knowing Scripture* (Downers Grove, Ill.: InterVarsity Press, 1977), 9–10.

3. The discussion of each of these elements in this lesson is necessarily brief. For a fuller discussion, see chapter 6 of my book, *A Book Like No Other: What's So Special About the Bible* (Phillipsburg, N.J.: P&R Publishing, 1998).

4. Quoted in Peter Lewis, *The Genius of Puritanism* (Carey Publications, 1977; reprint, Morgan, Pa.: Soli Deo Gloria, 1996), 54.

5. *Turning On the Light: Discovering the Riches of God's Word* will introduce you to enough basic study skills to get you

started on the road to responsible interpretation of Scripture. The "Recommended Reading" list in that book includes other books that will hone those basic skills.

6. R. C. Sproul, *Knowing Scripture* (Downers Grove, Ill.: InterVarsity Press, 1977), 17.

7. Maurice Roberts, "O the Depth!" *The Banner of Truth,* July 1990, 2. Quoted in Donald S. Whitney, *Spiritual Disciplines for the Christian Life* (Colorado Springs: NavPress, 1991), 55.

Exercises

Review

1. Compare the information revealed by a person's pulse with the information revealed by his or her love for the Word of God.

2. Explain the importance of consistent, balanced nourishment for both body and soul.

3. Describe in your own words Paul's command to "let the word of Christ richly dwell within you" (Colossians 3:16). Why does the Devil *not* want you to comply with Paul's command?

4. Read Nehemiah 8:6–8; Psalm 138:2; Luke 11:28; Ephesians 4:11–12; 1 Timothy 4:13; and 2 Timothy 4:2. Then explain the importance God places upon His people listening to His Word.

5. How can we overcome our culture's systematic destruction of our ability to read well? Why is it important for us to do so?

6. How does studying Scripture differ from reading Scripture? Describe three essential activities included in good study of Scripture.

7. Describe the importance of memorizing and meditating on Scripture.

Application

1. Evaluate your spiritual diet by examining the activities in which you are currently involved that get Scripture off the printed page and into your system. List each activity under these headings: Listening, Reading, Studying, Memorizing, Meditating. Now list the amount of time you spend each week on each activity. Based on your current activity, is your diet of Scripture consistent? Is it balanced? If not, what changes do you need to make in your diet? How will you implement these changes in your life? Who loves you enough to encourage you and hold you accountable for making these changes?

2. Review your memory verses from lessons 1–7. Begin memorizing one or more of the following:

   Luke 11:28
   Colossians 3:16
   1 Peter 5:8–9

Digging Deeper

1. Relate J. C. Ryle's quotation that opened this lesson to the words of J. I. Packer on pages 105–6.

9
The Exercise
of Obedience

*Let me be what I profess, do as well as teach, live as well
as hear religion.*   —From *The Valley of Vision:
A Collection of Puritan
Prayers and Devotions*

A̲s we turn our focus to the exercise of obedience, consider this modern-day parable:

*A woman in search of companionship for a long walk
sought out three of her friends. "Come, take a long walk with
me," she said to the first, who, with a deep sigh, responded,
"I would love to, my friend, but I have been so busy all day,
I've missed breakfast and lunch. I just don't have the energy
for a long walk."*

*The woman nodded in sympathy and approached her sec-
ond friend: "Won't you come with me on a long walk?" The
second friend yawned and rubbed her eyes in exhaustion.
"That sounds wonderful. But the baby kept me up most of the
night, and I need a nap." So the woman tucked her tired friend
into her cozy bed and went to the home of friend number three.*

"My dear friend, please get up off the couch and take a long walk with me." The third friend looked at the woman in utter amazement. "You can't be serious. You know I never go on long walks. I eat large heavy meals, retire early, rise late, and spend most of my day in front of the TV. If I were to walk past the corner, I'd probably drop dead from a heart attack or stroke!"

"Of course, you are right; I don't know what I was thinking," the woman replied as she set off on her walk, all by herself.

You may recall that a parable is a story designed to teach a particular point. When you read a parable, you should not try to make every element of the story "stand for" something as you would if you were reading an allegory. Rather, you should look for the particular point the storyteller wants to communicate. With that reminder in mind, go back and reread my "parable of the lone walker" in the light of the analogy we are developing in this study of spiritual strength. Then try to put the main point of the parable into a single sentence.

Here is how I would summarize the point of the parable: "Exercise is the centerpiece of a workout routine." If you came up with something different, just remember that it's *my* parable, and so I get the final word on its point! And if you don't quite see that point yet, perhaps I can make it clear by the end of this lesson.

The Centerpiece of Any Workout Routine
In previous lessons, we stressed the importance of a well-rounded workout routine in developing and maintaining physical and spiritual fitness. We indicated that a good

physical workout routine includes a consistent well-balanced diet, strenuous exercise, and rejuvenating rest. Then we drew the analogy that a good spiritual workout routine includes a consistent well-balanced diet of Scripture, the strenuous exercise of obedience, and the rejuvenating rest of prayer.

We saw that the *purpose* of "working out" spiritually is acquiring and maintaining the spiritual fitness we need to live out God's purposes for our salvation. We emphasized that the three essential ingredients of the workout routine work together to achieve an effective level of spiritual fitness. Now it is time to distinguish between the different roles the elements play in accomplishing that purpose.

Physical and spiritual fitness are actually *built up and strengthened* by the rigorous activity of strenuous exercise, while diet and rest *support* that activity with energizing nourishment and rejuvenating refreshment. Skipping meals when we're busy steals the energy we need to keep going, and lack of rest saps our strength for the work of the day. Good food and good rest are essential if we are to exercise well. However, they work against us when they are not combined with activity. An adequate (or more than adequate) diet accompanied by plenty of rest, but devoid of activity, produces ill-health and weakness instead of fitness and strength.

Thus, exercise is the centerpiece of any workout routine. Just as physical exercise is supported by good food and regular times of rest, so the spiritual exercise of obedience is supported by our intake of Scripture and regular times of prayer. And just as food and rest without exercise do a physical body more harm than good, so too Scripture intake and prayer without the exercise of obedience can actually damage our souls.

In our last lesson, we examined our intake of Scripture. In our next lesson we'll take a close look at the rest found in prayer. And in this lesson we focus on the centerpiece of our spiritual workout routine, the strenuous exercise of obedience to God.

The Grace of Salvation Produces Active Obedience

As a first step in examining the exercise of obedience, let's review the important relationship between God's grace and His law. Discussions of obedience are easily misunderstood when this relationship isn't clear, and such misunderstanding tends to fracture our fellowship and weaken us spiritually.

Simply put, no fallen sinner has ever been saved or will ever be saved by obeying the commands found in God's law, but that doesn't mean we are free to ignore them. God accomplished salvation when He graciously sent His Son Jesus Christ into the world for a dual purpose: (1) to provide perfect obedience to God's law, which would be credited as righteousness to God's chosen children, and (2) to atone for and satisfy God's righteous wrath against the sin of those children so that God could forgive them. Thus, salvation is wholly an act of God's grace.

If you are a Christian, it is because God chose to adopt you into His family before the foundation of the world and then accomplished His good pleasure for you through the work of His Son. You needed *both* righteousness and forgiveness to be accepted by God into His family, but in your sinful state, you could provide or merit neither. It took an act of God's mercy to provide them for you. Jesus' perfect life merited your righteousness before God, and His death for your sin assured your forgiveness. Salvation in Christ is thus necessarily a free gift from your Father God.

But the fact that salvation is free doesn't free you from the obligation to obey God's law. All creation is subject to

God's authority, and His law is an expression of that authority. Unsaved sinners will spend eternity in hell because of their disobedience to God's authority expressed in His law. Saved sinners will spend eternity in heaven, because they have been forgiven of their disobedience and given credit for the perfect obedience of Christ.

However, very few saved sinners go directly to heaven when they are saved. God leaves most us here in this fallen world for many years. And while we are here, He requires us to obey Him. His Word tells us why. We obey Him in this world for the praise of His glory and to "proclaim the excellencies of Him who has called us out of darkness into His marvelous light" (Ephesians 1:6, 12, 14; 1 Peter 2:9). A life of obedience does not secure our salvation; rather, it glorifies the God who saved us by grace.

Glorifying God is the ultimate purpose for which He saved us. We glorify God by revealing His character to those around us. God's law is a reflection of His perfect character because it expresses His will. Since His perfect character never changes, His will never changes. Therefore, His law cannot be set aside. The ceremonial aspects of His law expressed in the old covenant were completely *fulfilled* (not set aside) in the work of Christ. And the moral aspects of His law are still binding for new covenant Christians— not as the means of our salvation, but as the means of fulfilling the ultimate purpose of our salvation, the glorification of God.

Since we retain our depravity after salvation, we remain in need of God's grace as we strive to glorify Him by our obedience. And He remains faithful in providing it to us. He gives us His powerful indwelling Spirit to work in us as we expend the effort required to work out our salvation. Although God requires us to obey His commands, He expects us to do so in *His* strength, not ours. Thus as we emphasize the necessity of obedience in the lives of God's children, we are not preaching "another gospel" of salvation through good works. Rather we are preaching the *biblical* gospel of salvation unto good works that glorify God.

John MacArthur explains: "Our obedience does not *merit* salvation, of course. But genuine conversion to Christ inevitably produces obedience. Therefore, while obedience is never a *condition* for salvation, it is nonetheless always salvation's *fruit.* "[1] Michael Horton expresses it like this: "In Scripture . . . we are told to *believe* the gospel and *obey* the law, receiving God's favor from the one and God's guidance from the other. . . . Obedience must not be confused with the gospel. . . . The gospel *produces* new life, new experiences, and a new obedience."[2]

Both men echo the Bible's message that we are saved for the purpose of doing good works that glorify God in the midst of our fallen world. In Ephesians 2:8–10, Paul tells us that we are saved by grace through faith, and that no part of salvation comes from ourselves. However, as God's workmanship, we were "created in Christ Jesus for good works, which God prepared beforehand, that we should walk in them." And Jesus declared in Matthew 5:16 that He expects His followers to let their light shine before others in such a way that they may see His followers' good works and glorify God.

Salvation Is Not a Spectator Sport

Someone once described football as "twenty-two men on the field in desperate need of rest, being cheered on or put down by 60,000 fans in the stands desperately in need of exercise." Unfortunately, we could describe third-millennium Christians in much the same way. You know as well as I do that 90 percent of the work in most churches is done by 10 percent of the members. The other 90 percent of church members cheer on those hard workers, or put them down, without doing much work themselves. Thus, 10 percent of Christians could sure use some rest, while 90 percent of them could sure stand some exercise!

God never intended salvation to be a spectator sport. Arm-chair theologians, couch-potato Christians, and worship observers greatly abuse the precious gift their Father has given them. The Bible is clear that although God's gracious gift to His chosen children comes free of charge, it also comes with strings attached—make that *ropes* attached. Once we have freely received it, we are required to walk worthy of it.

Jesus urged His disciples to count the cost of following Him (Luke 14:28), but He also assured them that the cost, no matter how high, would be worth it (Mark 8:34–38). Walking worthy of our high calling in Christ is a strenuous activity that builds spiritual strength. The more actively we participate, the stronger and more effective we'll be in doing good works that glorify God. And the more faithful we are in doing the work He has called us to do, the greater will be our joy here on earth, and the more we will look forward to laying our heavenly crowns at our Savior's feet.

Scripture calls us to good works in three basic areas: our thinking, our attitudes, and our behavior. Paul tells us in Romans that because we have been united with Christ in His death and resurrection, we must consider ourselves "dead to sin" and not allow sin to reign in our mortal bodies (6:5–14). Rather, we are to present our bodies as living sacrifices, to reject conformity with the world, and to think with renewed minds in sound judgment (12:1–3).

In most of his shorter epistles, Paul gets a bit more specific. In Philippians he tells us to *think* about things that are true, honorable, right, pure, lovely, of good repute, excellent, and praiseworthy (4:8). In the same book, he exhorts us to imitate the *attitude* of humility and concern for the welfare of others that characterized Jesus (2:1–5). In Colossians he says, "Set your mind on the things above, not on the things that are on earth" (3:2), and, "See to it that no one takes you captive through philosophy and empty deception" (2:8). In Ephesians he tells us to be humble, gentle, and patient, being careful to preserve the unity of the Spirit in the bond of peace (4:2–3). And in all three of these letters, he includes lists of particular activities that should typify our behavior. (See Ephesians 4:25–6:19; Philippians 2:1–16; 4:4–9; Colossians 3:5–4:6.) Similar commands are sprinkled throughout his other epistles as well.

Paul understood that the exercise of obedience is indeed the centerpiece of our spiritual workout routine, and he wasn't shy about encouraging his readers to get up and get at it. And the very same kind of teaching is found in the writings of all the other New Testament authors. There is simply no way around it. Salvation is free, but it demands our obedience.

Obedience Is Acting in Jesus' Name

Most Christians, when faced with clear scriptural teaching about the importance of obedience, readily acknowledge their responsibility to obey God's commands. But far fewer Christians understand God's commands well enough to actually do them. That's why a good diet of Scripture is so important to the exercise of obedience. We simply can't *do* what we don't *know*.

One of the best "definitions" of obedience to God is found in Colossians 3:17. Immediately after exhorting us to let the word of Christ richly dwell within us, Paul says, "And whatever you do in word or deed, do all in the name of the Lord Jesus, giving thanks through Him to God the Father." I like this definition of obedience because it makes crystal clear the connection between knowing and doing.

When we let the Word settle down and be at home in our hearts, we'll know what to do, and we'll know how to do it. All aspects of our behavior will be carried out *in Jesus' name* with *gratitude* to God for the gift of salvation.

If you are familiar with *praying* in Jesus' name, you should easily grasp the concept of *behaving* in Jesus' name. Doing something in someone's name involves one of two things: either you do what he or she would do in the situation, or you do what he or she would want you to do in the situation. So, when we behave in Jesus' name, we either follow His example or we do His will for us.

The only way we can see His example and know His will for us is by studying Scripture. Acting on what we learn produces the kind of behavior in us that Jesus desires. That kind of behavior builds spiritual strength through regular, consistent strenuous exercise. As we grow stronger, we become better equipped to do God's work more effectively.

When we behave in Jesus' name while *giving thanks* for our salvation, we will be obeying God from the heart instead of merely externally. You are no doubt aware of several occasions in Scripture when a person was actually condemned for "obedience" devoid of a right heart attitude. And you may have wondered if obedience has any value at all if you don't want to do what God commands you to do.

If so, may I suggest that "not wanting to do what God commands you to do" doesn't necessarily mean that your heart isn't right. A right heart attitude is one that obeys out of gratitude for what God has done in our behalf, not *necessarily* one that is eager to act on a specific command.

As I see it, obedience that is acceptable to God occurs on at least three different levels. The first I would call "teeth-gritting" obedience; the second, "determined" obedience; and the third, "eager" obedience. The first is motivated almost entirely by duty, which, although not the best motive, is not a bad motive either. Obedience in response to a sense of duty acknowledges God's sovereign authority and His right to rule His creation. This sense of duty is often shot through with gratitude for what God has done even when it is not drenched in desire to do what is commanded.

The third level, "eager" obedience, is motivated almost entirely by joyous love for God. Obedience at this level is easy because we really enjoy it. Of course, this is the very best motive for obeying God, because it reflects His glory best in our fallen world.

The second level of "determined obedience" can fall anywhere between those two extremes. It has moved beyond "doing it simply because God is the Boss" but has not yet arrived at "doing it in sheer joy." We are at the point where we *want* to obey God, although we may not delight in doing what He has commanded. This is the level where most of us seem to be most of the time.

Christians can and should obey at all of these levels *with grateful hearts.* When we focus on obeying (even at level one) with thanksgiving, we will find ourselves moving on to levels two and three more and more often. Of course, God is most glorified with eager obedience that flows out of His children's joyous love for Him. But "eager" obedience doesn't just happen; it requires a great deal of spiritual strength. That is one reason why we should work hard at developing and maintaining a good spiritual workout routine. The strenuous exercise of obedience, nourished by Scripture and rejuvenated by prayer, builds the spiritual fitness we need to glorify God through our eager response to His will.

Notes

1. John MacArthur, "Obedience: Love or Legalism?" in *Trust and Obey: Obedience and the Christian,* ed. Rev. Don Kistler (Morgan, Pa.: Soli Deo Gloria, 1996), 50.

2. Michael Horton, "Filthy Rags or Perfect Righteousness" in *Trust and Obey: Obedience and the Christian,* ed. Rev. Don Kistler (Morgan, Pa.: Soli Deo Gloria, 1996), 39–41.

Exercises

Review

1. In your own words, *briefly* explain the idea that exercise is the centerpiece of a workout routine. Be sure to include a description of the role played by each essential element of a workout routine, and to draw the analogy between physical and spiritual workout routines.

2. How did God accomplish the salvation of His chosen children through the work of His Son, Jesus Christ? (Hint: Consider what we fallen sinners needed to be reconciled to God, and how the work of Christ accomplished that need.)

3. Demonstrate from Scripture that receiving the free gift of salvation does not free us from the obligation of obeying God's law. (Hint: Consider the purpose of salvation, and how Christians fulfill that purpose.)

4. Read Mark 8:34–38; Luke 14:28; Romans 6:5–14; 12:1–3; and Ephesians 4:1. Then describe the "strings" that are attached to salvation. Do these "strings" seem more like ropes to you? Why or why not?

5. In what three basic areas are we called to do good works? Give several examples from Scripture of specific good works in each of these areas.

6. Explain in your own words the excellent definition of obedience to God found in Colossians 3:17. Then read

this verse in the context of Colossians 3:16–4:6 and explain the *practical* relationship between Bible study, prayer, and obedience that is depicted in that passage.

Application

1. Describe the three "levels" of obedience described in this lesson. Then divide a piece of paper into three columns and label the columns with the three levels of obedience. Under each heading, list specific acts of obedience that you typically perform at each level. Which column is longer? In the light of this exercise, meditate on John 14:15–24 and 1 John 2:3–6. Then think carefully about what your usual level of obedience tells you about your love for God. Do you need to cultivate a deeper love for Him? If so, how will you do this? Make a specific plan that will help you cultivate this deeper love. Then share your plan with someone who loves you enough to encourage you and hold you accountable.

2. Read Romans 6; Romans 12; Ephesians 4:17–6:20; and Colossians 3:1–4:6. Drawing upon one or more of those passages, list three or more specific acts of obedience in the areas of your thinking, your attitudes, and your behavior that need to be strengthened. Prayerfully choose one to begin working on this week. Then describe what specific actions you will take to strengthen this area of your life.

3. Review your memory verses from previous lessons. Then begin memorizing one or more of the following:

   Romans 12:1–3
   Colossians 3:17
   1 Peter 2:9

Digging Deeper

1. Which do you think is more important in obeying God: a sense of duty, or a sense of love? Explain your answer thoroughly, supporting your thinking with Scripture.

10

The Rejuvenating
Rest of Prayer

There can be no security felt unless we satisfy ourselves
of the truth of a divine superintendence and can com-
mit our lives and all that we have into the hands of God.
The first thing which we must look to is His power, that
we may have a thorough conviction of His being a sure
refuge to such as cast themselves upon His care. With
this there must be conjoined confidence in His mercy,
to prevent those anxious thoughts which might other-
wise rise in our minds.　　　　　—John Calvin

Hard work makes me tired. And I expect that it has the
same effect on you. That's because you and I are both
fallen sinners, and fatigue in hard work was part of God's
curse upon sinful humanity. In Genesis 3:16–19, God told
our first parents that because of their sin, the labor God had
designed as a blessed privilege for them would henceforth
be undertaken in pain, toil, and sweat. Thus, it is not hard
work itself that came from God's curse, but the physical fatigue and mental frustration that accompany it now.

God designed us for work. He created Adam and Eve and put them in the Garden of Eden "to cultivate it and keep it" (2:15). I'm sure they worked very hard to care for that Garden, but Scripture gives no indication that their work was exhausting—until they defied God by their disobedience. From that moment on, the pleasure of hard, useful work has been tainted by fatigue and frustration.

But God's curse on human sin was accompanied by His glorious promise of redemption and rest. Those He had chosen for adoption into His family would be freed from the effects of the curse through the work of God's Son. Full freedom would be progressive instead of immediate and would equip the elect to live out their Father's purpose for their salvation.

At the moment of their adoption they would be freed from the futility of living under the *penalty* for sin. As they worked out their salvation in a fallen world, they would be freed from the stress of being bound by the *power* of sin. And when they were finally taken home to live with their Father forever, they would rest free from the very *presence* of sin.

God's grace and mercy are well reflected in His great promise of redemption and rest. Though no fallen sinner deserves anything more than God's just condemnation, some of us have been blessed to receive unmerited pardon. But because that pardon is purposeful, it brings with it the requirement of hard, useful work.

We have seen in previous lessons that God's call to salvation is a call to action. We have also seen that performing that action well involves strenuous spiritual exercise fueled by a good diet of Scripture. We have mentioned that strenuous spiritual exercise must be frequently rejuvenated by periods of spiritual rest. As we work our way through this lesson, we will see how God revives our ability to act in obedience by giving us frequent tastes here on earth of the ultimate rest we will have when we get to heaven. We savor the flavor of that ultimate rest when we seek our Father's close company through the family privilege of prayer.

Work Hard Now, Rest Well Later

Hebrews 4 makes it clear that God intends for us to work hard now and rest well later—at least in an ultimate sense. In that passage the writer emphasizes God's glorious promise of an eventual "Sabbath rest for the people of God," and then admonishes us to "be diligent to enter that rest, lest anyone fall through following the same example of disobedience" (vv. 1–11). The "same example of disobedience" that we are to reject is that of those who had the Good News preached to them but failed to profit from it because their hearing "was not united by faith" (vv. 2–3). When we reject their foolish example by being diligent in believing, we enter God's rest through the door opened for us by Jesus Christ. In verses 14–16, the writer of Hebrews encourages those of us who believe to avail ourselves of that rest:

> Since then we have a great high priest who has passed through the heavens, Jesus the Son of God, let us hold fast our confession. For we do not have a high priest who cannot sympathize with our weaknesses, but one who has been tempted in all things as we are, yet without sin. Let us therefore draw near with confidence to the throne of grace, that we may receive mercy and may find grace to help in time of need.

The work of Jesus Christ not only assures us of "Sabbath rest" in eternity, but it also qualifies us to draw near to God's throne of grace now. There at His feet we can rest in His mercy and draw strength from His promise of help available for all of our needs. God knows that those who work hard need to rest well. And since He requires His children to work hard in His service, He blesses them with the rest they need *here and now* to accomplish the tasks He has set before them.

Interestingly, it is those who work hardest who seem to rest best. Think of it in physical terms for a moment. When do you sleep and rest best? When you have been lounging around all day watching TV? Or when you have been engaged for long hours in strenuous physical labor? Most of us have experienced the irritation of having lain around all day not doing much, feeling absolutely worn out by all that inactivity, only to drop into bed and be unable to sleep! We all seem to sleep better when we've been very active.

Spiritual rest seems to work in much the same way. When we "lie around" in God's service not doing much, we may feel the need for the refreshment of prayer, but when we drop to our knees, we're unable to focus. Rejuvenation in prayer seems to flow most freely and fully from the exhaustion of service. Perhaps that is why Paul exhorts us to be *devoted* to prayer.

Devotion to Prayer Is Devotion to Rest

Paul told the Colossians, "Devote yourselves to prayer, keeping alert in it with an attitude of thanksgiving" (4:2). The New King James Version translates his thought this way: "Continue earnestly in prayer, being vigilant in it with thanksgiving." Now that may not sound, at first hearing, as if he is speaking of rest—but he really is.

One of the reasons I look forward to the Sabbath each week is that I am *devoted* to rest. I anticipate *continuing earnestly* in rest for one day in seven. When I hop out of bed on Sunday morning (Yes, I am one of those disgusting morning people!), I am filled with thanksgiving for another opportunity to *keep alert* and *be vigilant* in the task of resting in the Lord for a whole day.

The point I am trying to make here is that rest is not always equivalent to inactivity. Although my Sabbath day rest usually includes an afternoon nap, it is primarily consumed with restful *activities*. Worship, reading, listening to music, talking with family and friends, and taking leisurely contemplative walks are all active pursuits that bring rest to my soul and to my body.

Prayer is also a spiritually and physically restful *activity* that demands an alert mind, a grateful heart, and devotion of will. We need to *think* when we pray. Paul told the Corinthians to pray with their minds as well as "with the spirit" (1 Corinthians 14:15). How do we apply his exhortation today? By simultaneously letting God's Word dwell in us richly and being filled with His Spirit (Colossians 3:16; Ephesians 5:18). Setting our minds on Scripture and seeking understanding and wisdom from the Holy Spirit generates confident prayer in God's will. Such prayers give us rest because we know they'll be answered (see 1 John 5:14–15).

We must also approach prayer with an *attitude of thanksgiving* to God for His mercy and grace. The best way to soak prayer in gratitude is to begin with reminders of God's attributes and His actions in our behalf (for a good example, see Acts 4:24–26), and then to proceed immediately to confession of sin (see Daniel 9:4–19). When we initiate prayer in that manner, we will see ourselves rightly as undeserving of all God has accomplished in our behalf to the praise of His glory, and we will be thankful for what He has done.

When our minds are engaged with God's truth and our hearts are rejoicing with gratitude, our *wills* surrender more easily to God's purposes for us. A Spirit-led understanding of God's person and work accompanied by humble thanksgiving for the many ways He has blessed us quickly breaks down our resistance to willful obedience.

Prayer's Restful Activity Prepares Us for Service

When we actively pray with alert minds, grateful hearts, and surrendered wills, we'll come away rested, refreshed, and rejuvenated—ready for another strenuous round of spiritual exercise. Prayer affects us that way for at least three very good reasons: (1) It acknowledges our complete dependence on God's grace and power in every aspect of life; (2) It helps us to focus on seeking *first* His kingdom and righteousness; and (3) It reminds us of His promises to meet our every need in working out our salvation.

Restful prayer follows the perfect pattern for prayer that Jesus gave His disciples to pass on to us. Read this prayer pattern carefully and think about how it encourages rest.

> Pray, then, in this way:
> Our Father who art in heaven,
> Hallowed be Thy name.
> Thy kingdom come.
> Thy will be done,
> On earth as it is in heaven.
> Give us this day our daily bread.
> And forgive us our debts, as we also have
> forgiven our debtors.
> And do not lead us into temptation, but deliver
> us from evil. [For Thine is the kingdom, and
> the power, and the glory, forever. Amen.]
> (Matthew 6:9–13)[1]

Did you see that this prayer pattern falls into two distinct sections? The first calls us to set our minds, hearts, and wills squarely on God and His purposes, and the second exhorts us *then* to seek from Him everything we need to work out His purposes for our salvation. Jesus gave us this pattern for prayer because He knew that the Father intended our prayers to be a key means of rejuvenation for spiritual service. The refreshment we need to walk worthy of our high calling comes from resting in God—not from rehearsing our worries and selfish desires. When we *first* focus on God and His purposes, we will see our concerns in the context of God's powerful, purposeful care. And that gives us rest.

With that thought in mind, go back and read carefully the words of John Calvin that opened this lesson. I think Calvin understood that devotion to prayer comes naturally when we are devoted to resting in God. And that devotion to rest comes naturally to those who work hard in God's service. Those who work hard need to rest well; and those who work hardest seem to rest best. When God's children grow weary in doing good, they find the refreshment they need in God-focused prayer.

John Calvin's description of our rest in God's care reminds me of the way a child who has been frightened by a storm will calm down and sleep in Mom or Dad's arms. The storm is still raging outside, but the child is at rest. That's the way we should rest when we are embraced by our Father in times of prayer.

Notes

1. For an deeper discussion of this marvelous prayer pattern, see chapter 12 of the Light for Your Path study, *Before the Throne of God: Focus on Prayer* (Phillipsburg, N.J.: P&R Publishing, 1999).

Exercises

Review

1. Read Genesis 2–3 and explain the effect of God's curse upon the hard, useful work Adam and Eve were designed to do. How should God's accompanying promise of redemption and rest (Genesis 3:15) influence our attitude toward work?

2. Explain the relationship between the rejuvenating rest of prayer and the eventual Sabbath rest God has promised His people (see Hebrews 4).

3. Paul instructs us to "devote" ourselves to prayer (to "continue earnestly" in it) and to keep "alert" (to be "vigilant") in prayer. How do these words, which imply strenuous effort, encourage rest? Describe at least three activities that are involved in the process of resting in prayer.

4. Read the prayer of the Jerusalem believers recorded in Acts 4:24–30, and the prayer of Daniel recorded in Daniel 9:4–19. Although neither of these prayers contains specific expressions of thanksgiving to God, certain attitudes expressed in both of them stimulate gratitude toward God in the hearts of those praying. Identify these attitudes and explain how they stimulate gratitude.

5. List at least three ways in which the rejuvenating rest of prayer prepares us for another strenuous round of spiritual exercise. Then explain how patterning our prayers after Jesus' words in Matthew 6:9–13 will help us rest well in prayer so that we can work hard in God's service.

Application

1. Do you currently consider your times of prayer as a primary means of resting well enough to become rejuvenated for service? If you answered yes, explain how your times of prayer rejuvenate you for service. Give specific examples to support your assertions. If you answered no, describe one or more insights you received from this lesson that could help you rest well through prayer. What changes in your daily routine must you make to implement these insights as part of your prayer times? When will you begin making these changes? Who loves you enough to hold you accountable? When will you ask them to do so?

2. If you do not have Matthew 6:9–13 committed to memory, write it out on a card and keep it "before your face" when you pray. For the next week, consciously focus upon praying according to the priorities found in this pattern for prayer. That is, first seek God's honor, glory, and purposes, and then seek from God the resources you need to do the work He has called you to do. At the end of the week evaluate whether this conscious prayer focus has helped you to rest in prayer and to be rejuvenated for service. If it has, explain why you think it has done so.

3. Review your memory verses from previous lessons. Then begin memorizing one or more of the following:

   Genesis 3:15
   Colossians 4:2
   Hebrews 4:14–16
   1 John 5:14–15

Digging Deeper

1. Read carefully the words of John Calvin that introduce this lesson in the light of what you have learned about the rejuvenating rest of prayer. Then write a few concise paragraphs explaining ways in which resting in prayer contributes to (1) feelings of security, (2) conviction of God's being a sure refuge, and (3) confidence in God's mercy.

PART 4

Three Devious Strength Stealers

11

Laziness

The Christian ideal has not been tried and found wanting. It has been found difficult and left untried.

—G. K. Chesterton

If you are a sports fan (as I am), you know that success in athletic contests usually requires both a good offense and a good defense. And if you are also a fan of the apostle Paul (as I am) you know that he often compared the Christian life to athletic competition.

You'll remember, of course, how he encouraged the Christians in Corinth to "run in such a way that you may win" and thereby receive an imperishable wreath (1 Corinthians 9:24–25). And how he summarized his own ministry in terms of "press[ing] on toward the goal for the prize of the upward call of God in Christ Jesus" (Philippians 3:14). And how, at the end of that great ministry, he exhorted his young protégé Timothy to compete as an athlete who must play by the rules if he desires to win the prize (2 Timothy 2:5).

In each of those instances, Paul was using athletics to make a spiritual point. Just as athletes prepare themselves to compete and win against daunting opponents, Christians must also prepare themselves in order to overcome the fiercest opponent of all.

This study of spiritual strength focuses on that necessary preparation. No right-thinking athlete would enter an arena without adequate training, because to do so would mean almost certain defeat. Such a foolish athlete could only hope that his opponent had come even less prepared.

But if there is one thing that Christians can be sure of, it is that their opponent *never* arrives unprepared. Scripture tells us to be "on the alert" because our "adversary, the devil, prowls about like a roaring lion, seeking someone to devour" (1 Peter 5:8). Competing *so as to win* against such an opponent requires a great deal of spiritual strength. And great spiritual strength comes and grows only through the intense preparation of both a good offense and a good defense.

The lessons we have studied thus far have focused upon the *offensive effort* required to build strength. If you have worked through them with us, you know that a good offense involves "working out" with the raw materials God freely gave you when He adopted you into His family. You'll remember that those raw materials include the life of salvation, the good bones of knowledge, the muscles of faith, the blood of love, and the skin of fellowship. And you'll understand that simply having those raw materials in your possession won't make you spiritually strong in God's service. You must also put them to work to help you digest a consistent balanced diet of Scripture, exercise strenuously through obedience to God, and seek rejuvenation and refreshment in prayer.

The final three lessons before us concern the defensive effort required to build spiritual strength. If we want to compete *so as to win* against the world, the flesh, and the Devil, we must prepare ourselves to defend against four devious strength stealers: laziness, neglect, disease, and injury. In this lesson we will consider the strength stealer of laziness. In lesson 12, we will look at some ways in which neglect saps strength. And in lesson 13, we will focus on the traumatic affects of spiritual disease and injury.

Both the offensive and defensive activities required to build strength demand that we set our minds on the things above instead of the things on the earth. To build strength, both offensively and defensively, we must look to the exalted, preeminent Christ, who exercises all authority from the right hand of God (Matthew 28:18; Acts 2:33–36). He, and He alone, is the source of the strength we will need to foil our fierce opponent.

Peter, Watch Where You're Looking!

Peter learned this lesson vividly one night during a hair-raising storm on the Sea of Galilee. Jesus had sent His disciples ahead of Him to the other side of the lake, and during the crossing the boat was hit by sudden contrary winds and battering waves. While the disciples were struggling to save their boat and their lives, Jesus "came to them, walking on the sea" (Matthew 14:25). The men were afraid, thinking He was a ghost. But Jesus revealed His identity and told them to take courage. Peter wasted no time in complying: "Lord, if it is You, command me to come to You on the water," he said. And Jesus said, "Come!" (vv. 28–29).

Peter knew that he couldn't obey that command unless his Lord gave him the power to do it. The only way Peter would be able to walk on stormy seas toward his Master was by looking to Jesus for strength to obey His command. Peter was "strong in God's service" as long as his eyes remained firmly fixed on his Lord.

But Peter was so very much like you and me. In no time at all, he shifted his gaze from his Savior to "the things of this earth"—the waves, the wind, the water, and his own inability. At that very moment, Peter sank like a rock—like the weak rock he was *at that very moment*. Peter wasn't a goner, however. His name didn't appear in the obituary column of the *Tiberias Gazette* the next morning. He knew where to find the strength that he needed to overcome his own failure. He cried out to Jesus for help, and the Lord graciously saved him.

When we face distressing assaults from the world, the flesh, and the Devil, we will also be tempted to let our eyes slip from our Lord to the things of the earth. When we succumb to those temptations, we will lose the strength that we need to walk worthy of our high calling in Christ. But because we are children of God, all is not lost. The energizing strength that we need will once more surge through our souls the moment we call out to our gracious Lord for His assistance.

Defending Against Assaults of Laziness

If you know very much about Paul, you know he was *not* a lazy apostle! I find it hard to believe that Paul ever struggled with laziness. Unfortunately however, most of us do. So what can we learn from his life and letters in the New Testament that will help us defend our souls against those inevitable deadly assaults from our own lazy flesh?

Paul's energetic, hard-working example of service to God was characterized by the great effort he poured into ministry, and by his frequent admonitions to Christians to work hard at their calling. In Colossians 1:28–29, Paul captures the essence of his life's consuming mission: "And we proclaim Him, admonishing every man and teaching every man with all wisdom, that we may present every man complete in Christ. And for this purpose also I labor, striving according to His power, which mightily works within me." Interestingly, Paul uses words like "labor" and "striving" to describe his service to God. Obviously, ministry wasn't something Paul did in his spare time. It wasn't something he worked into his schedule when he wasn't too busy. Nor was it something he got around to at the end of week if he wasn't too tired. Ministry, for Paul, was *labor*—labor that required *striving*.

The Greek word translated "striving" in verse 29 is a form of *agōnizomai,* which means "fight" or "wrestle." It implies struggle against opposition and has given us our English word "agonize." Clearly, striving and laziness are incompatible. Lazy people don't strive to do much of anything, because they cherish comfort. Cherishing comfort indulges the flesh, and indulging the flesh encourages laziness. It's a vicious circle.

When we cherish comfort, we don't want to do anything that doesn't come easy. When we hear Jesus say, "Take up your cross and follow me," we decide that He meant, "Hang a lovely gold ornament around your neck and stroll with Me along pleasant pathways." When we cherish our comfort, we hear Him wrongly. And when we hear Him wrongly, we don't obey Him.

The cross He had in mind was not a lovely gold ornament, but one upon which we crucify self and exalt our God. Following Him seldom leads us down pleasant pathways, but more often through rugged terrain. Taking up that cross and following Him requires a commitment to *striving*—to fighting, wrestling, and struggling against the opposition we get from our lazy, comfort-cherishing flesh. If we want to walk worthy of our high calling in Christ, we simply can't cherish our comfort above the pursuit of God's kingdom.

No Better Example Than Paul's

To learn how to pursue the kingdom above our own comfort, we couldn't ask for a better example than Paul's. His devotion to God overwhelmed his devotion to comfort and spawned his willingness "to endure all things for the sake of those who are chosen" (2 Timothy 2:10). Paul didn't consider it a hardship to count all things as loss in view of the surpassing value of knowing Christ Jesus. And he did not feel deprived when required to turned his back on worldly prestige and power in order to lay hold of that for which his Lord had laid hold of him (Philippians 3:7–14).

Paul's walk with the Lord took him through treacherous journeys, savage beatings, stonings, shipwrecks, and imprisonment. He regularly faced hostility and opposition from Gentiles, his own countrymen, and false brethren. He was well acquainted with sleeplessness, hunger and thirst, cold and exposure. And he carried at all times a crushing burden of concern for the welfare of all the churches he had been instrumental in founding. Amazingly, he described these kinds of circumstances as "momentary, light affliction" (2 Corinthians 4:17)!

Paul's Christian life was far from comfortable, but he did not set his mind on the things of this earth. You may remember how he described for the Philippians the driving force of his life. He said, "Forgetting what lies behind and reaching forward to what lies ahead, I press on toward the goal for the prize of the upward call of God in Christ Jesus" (3:13–14). Paul knew that the labor required to "present every man complete in Christ" required him to "press on" in the midst of great difficulties. He also knew that the strength he would need to live so intensely came solely from "fixing [his] eyes on Jesus, the author and perfecter of [his] faith, who for the joy set before Him endured the cross, despising the shame, and has sat down at the right hand of the throne of God" (Hebrews 12:2).

Jim Elliot, the well-known martyred missionary, under-stood and shared Paul's commitment to ministering with his eyes fixed squarely on Jesus—and he captured the mo-tivation behind their shared focus when he wrote in his journal, "He is no fool who gives what he cannot keep to gain what he cannot lose."[1]

The Secret of Commitment

What is the secret of that kind of intense commitment? We third-millennium Christians seem to be so preoccupied with our comfort that few of us live the way Paul did. How-ever, walking worthy of our high calling in Christ demands that we break the grip of that addiction. It won't be easy, but it must be done.

Let's look at how we can strive against laziness in Chris-tian service by looking again at how Paul described his own striving in service. In Colossians 1:29, he said that his la-bor of presenting every man complete in Christ involved "striving *according to His power,* which mightily works within me." Paul was not laboring in his own strength! He was striving *according to* the power of God that worked mightily within him.

We've already discussed the phrase "according to" and contrasted it to the phrase "out of." And you may recall that we said a billionaire who gives one hundred dollars to your favorite charity gives *out of* his wealth, but when he gives you one million dollars, he gives *according to* his wealth. When we first used that example, we were looking at Paul's prayer for the Colossians to be strengthened *according to* God's glorious might. Now we see that Paul's prayer for them was grounded in his own personal experience. His own striving in ministry was empowered *according to* the mighty working of God's power within him.

Paul knew he was too weak in himself to do God's work

in God's way. But he also knew that as a child of God, he had access to the inestimable power of God, and that all of that power was at his disposal to accomplish the work God had called him to do. He had, after all, told the Corinthians that "God is able to make all grace abound to you, that always having all sufficiency in everything, you may have an abundance for every good deed" (2 Corinthians 9:8).

Paul knew the great joy and confidence of relying on God's mighty power, because he had lived through the futility of relying on self. Paul was no weakling when God "reached out and touched him" on the road to Damascus. He was a powerful, resourceful, committed, prestigious hater of Christians. And God wisely weakened him to get his attention.

Perfected in Weakness— The Essence of Strength

God did that by blinding Paul's eyes in order to enlighten his heart. This once indomitable emissary of hate spent three days in a physical darkness that allowed him to see clearly, for the very first time, his own sinful hopelessness and the glory of Christ's work of redemption.

God sent a frightened believer named Ananias to restore Paul's physical sight and to commission him as God's chosen instrument to take His truth to the Gentiles (Acts 9:10–15). God then proceeded to use His chosen instrument in mighty ways. Paul received revelations of surpassing value from God, saw much fruit produced from his itinerant ministry, and was privileged to write much of the New Testament. From what we know of his preconversion personality (which God transformed, but did not destroy), we can safely surmise that Paul must have been frequently tempted to exalt himself and to fall back into ingrained habits of self-reliance. However, God kept His chosen instrument usefully humble by blessing him with a physical weakness that He refused to remove in spite of Paul's earnest prayers.

I believe one of the reasons God chose *not* to remove Paul's "thorn in the flesh" was to keep his eyes fixed squarely on Christ instead of on the things of the earth. I also believe that God's Holy Spirit then led Paul to record in Scripture the hard lesson he'd learned as exhortation for us to do the same thing. In 2 Corinthians 12:7–10, Paul tells us,

> Because of the surpassing greatness of the revelations, for this reason, to keep me from exalting myself, there was given me a thorn in the flesh, a messenger of Satan to buffet me—to keep me from exalting myself!
>
> Concerning this I entreated the Lord three times that it might depart from me. And He has said to me, "My grace is sufficient for you, for power is perfected in weakness."
>
> Most gladly, therefore, I will rather boast about my weaknesses, that the power of Christ may dwell in me. Therefore I am well content with weaknesses, with insults, with distresses, with persecutions, with difficulties, for Christ's sake; for when I am weak, then I am strong.

Paul's God-given physical weakness (whatever it was) distressed him enough to drive him to his knees on three separate occasions. Living with it was not something Paul wanted to do. But when God said to him, "You will be stronger in service to Me with it than without it," Paul said, "In that case, I will gladly keep it." His attitude speaks volumes about what was most important to Paul. He characteristically cherished God's purposes for him above his own comfort. That is why he could *rejoice* in proclaiming, "I can do all things through Him who strengthens me" (Philippians 4:13).

He knew firsthand that God does supply all of our needs in His service *according to* (there's that phrase again) His riches in glory (v. 19). The apostle's submissive contentment became a means for displaying God's glory and for growing in joy. His humble acceptance of God's perfect provision shifted the eyes of the world from Paul's great abilities to those of his God.

Paul honestly acknowledged that ministry was a struggle. He wanted the Colossians to know "how great a struggle" he had on their behalf (2:1)—and that the struggle was well worth the effort. He would have pronounced a hearty "Amen!" to the words of J. C. Ryle when he said, "If there is anything that deserves a struggle in this world, it is prosperity of the soul."[2]

Prosperity of soul requires deep knowledge of Christ in whom, Paul said, "are hidden all the treasures of wisdom and knowledge" (2:3). Digging for such valuable treasure involves a lot of hard work and cannot be done with a focus on worldly comfort. If we want to possess it, we would do well to imitate Paul by striving, *according to* God's mighty power, to fix our focus on the things that are above instead of the things on the earth.

Notes

1. Elisabeth Elliot, *Shadow of the Almighty* (San Francisco: Harper and Row, 1958), 108.

2. J. C. Ryle, *Practical Religion* (1878; reprint, Carlisle, Pa.: Banner of Truth, 1998), 31.

Exercises

Review

1. Briefly explain the importance of having both a good offense and a good defense in athletic contests. Read 1 Corinthians 9:24–27; Philippians 3:8–14; 2 Timothy 2:5; and 1 Peter 5:6–11. Then apply your understanding of the importance of a good offense and a good defense in sports to walking worthy of your high calling in Christ.

2. How does Peter's experience with Christ in a storm on the Sea of Galilee illustrate our need to apply Colossians 3:1–2 to building and maintaining spiritual strength? Do you know of any other good scriptural illustrations of this crucial truth? If so, describe one or more of them also.

3. Describe in your own words the essence of Paul's life-consuming mission (see Colossians 1:28–29). According to Paul, what was the basic purpose of his ministry? Do you agree that he considered this to be a "life-consuming" task? Explain.

4. Define and explain the significance of the following words and phrases that Paul uses in Colossians 1:28–29:

   labor:
   striving:
   according to:

5. Read 2 Corinthians 4:1–18; 11:16–12:10; Philippians 3:7–14; and 2 Timothy 2:1–10. Drawing on what you learn about Paul in these verses, explain why we would be hard pressed to find a better example of pursuing God's kingdom above our own comfort.

6. What is the secret of the kind of intense commitment to kingdom service that leaves no room in our lives for spiritual laziness?

7. In 2 Corinthians 12:7–10, Paul expresses a change of heart. First describe the change of heart he expresses and then explain in your own words what motivated his change of heart.

Application

1. Do you think there is a difference between *enjoying* comfort and *cherishing* comfort? Explain your answer using examples from your own life or from the lives of people in Scripture.

    a. In the light of your previous answer, list several ways in which third-millennium Christians *cherish* their comfort.

    b. To which items on your list are you personally prone?

    c. Do the ways in which you are prone to cherish your comfort interfere with your pursuit of God's kingdom? Explain, giving specific examples.

    d. Prayerfully consider the changes you should make in your attitudes and behavior that will give you more energy to walk worthy of your high calling in Christ. List one or more of those changes and make a plan to begin implementing at least one of them this week.

2. What have you learned from Paul's example in this lesson that has encouraged you to begin defending against the assault of laziness in your walk with the Lord? How will you apply what you have learned? Answer specif-

ically, remembering that a specific answer addresses the questions, Who? What? When? Where? and How?

3. Review your memory verses from previous lessons. Then begin memorizing one or more of the following:

   2 Corinthians 12:9–10
   Philippians 3:13–14
   2 Timothy 2:10

Digging Deeper

1. Relate the following quotations and explain how the two taken together summarize the message of lesson 11.

   If there is anything that deserves a struggle in this world, it is prosperity of the soul. (J. C. Ryle)

   The Christian ideal has not been tried and found wanting. It has been found difficult and left untried. (G. K. Chesterton)

12
Neglect

Whatever darkens our views or shakes our confidence with respect to any of the great principles of our Christian faith, cuts the very sinews of dutiful exertion, so that it becomes very difficult, or rather altogether impossible, to persevere in running "the race that is set before us." —John Brown

Neglect may well be the most devious stealer of strength. And if you have ever embarked on a physical workout routine to build strength, you know that already. Neglect is so devious because it requires no effort at all. We don't have to think about it, plan it, or do it. The only requirement for achieving neglect is—nothing at all. Perhaps that is why so many structured workout routines come with an intriguing array of motivational materials! The folks who design them know (from personal experience) the value of guarding against this devious strength stealer.

Neglect does its dastardly work in a number of ways, the most popular being procrastination. It usually goes something like this: *I'll start tomorrow, or next week, or next month, or after the holidays.* But sometimes it sounds more like this: *Wow, I did so much good strength-building work yesterday, I think I'll take today off—and maybe tomorrow too.* And once in a while it sounds like this: *You know, I just don't think I'm ready to actually start doing anything yet. I need to spend more time (hopefully a lot more) learning the theory behind all this workout stuff before I start doing it.*

Most of us recognize excuses for procrastination when we hear them, and given the right motivation, we can overcome them. A woman once told me that her husband was having difficulty getting out of bed in the morning. I asked her if she thought he could overcome his procrastination if the bed were on fire. She suddenly realized that all he needed was the right motivation. We're all like that man. Procrastination is easily conquered when we see a real need to get up and get moving.

However, the devious strength stealer of neglect won't be defeated that easily. It stands ready to launch a deadly counterattack against those who finally get motivated. This attack can steal strength just as effectively as procrastination, but it is less easily recognized as an attack. It takes the form of encouraging *lopsided effort*. Lopsided effort steals strength by emphasizing some elements of a good workout routine at the expense of others.

The Combination of Elements Builds Strength

As we saw earlier, it is the wise combination of well-balanced nutrition, strenuous exercise, and rejuvenating rest that builds strength. Lopsided effort upsets the proportions of that combination and produces weakness.

I'm sure you're aware of what happens to our bodies when we eat well, but never exercise—or when we exercise strenuously without proper nourishment—or when we either rest all the time or don't rest enough. You don't have to be a physical fitness expert to understand the importance of properly combining nutrition, exercise, and rest. Those who eat well and rest well but exercise poorly (or not at all) soon grow fat, lazy, and weak. And those who exercise mightily without proper nutrition and rest end up exhausted, injured, or sick.

The same kind of unhappy results await Christians who engage in lopsided *spiritual* workout routines. Those who devote all their time to Bible study and prayer while neglecting the exercise of obedience become puffed up with pride, arrogant toward others, and practically worthless in a crisis. On the other hand, those who are so consumed with spiritual busyness that they neglect Bible study and prayer end up pursuing wrong goals, growing more and more legalistic, and heading directly for burnout without passing "GO" and collecting two hundred dollars.

So, if we want to walk worthy of our high calling in Christ (and we do!), we need to *work hard* at maintaining the right combination of those spiritual disciplines. Paul told the Colossians to "let the word of Christ richly dwell within [them]" (3:16)—in other words, *work hard* at Bible study. He also said, "Whatever you do in word or deed, do *all* in the name of the Lord Jesus" (3:17)—in other words, *work hard* at obedience. And he exhorted them to devote themselves to prayer, "keeping alert in it with an attitude of thanksgiving" (4:2)—in other words, *work hard* at prayer.

Paul's emphasis on working hard at *all three* of those essential activities implies the importance of guarding against lopsided effort. He knew how prone we all are to excuse our neglect of one or two of those areas because we work so hard at the others. Most Christians, at some point in their walk with the Lord, have said things like, "I spend so much time studying the Bible that I don't have much time for prayer."

Or, "I feel so guilty when I sit down to study or pray because there is so much work that needs to be done." Or, "Prayer *is* the work God has given me to do." Or, "God reveals His will to me when I pray, so I don't need to study the Bible."

Paul knew that statements like these reflect neglect of essential spiritual disciplines—neglect that seriously weakens the speaker's ability to serve God effectively. Paul wants us to guard against such neglect so that we can be strong in God's service instead. He wants us to be alert to the dangers of pharisaical Bible study void of earnest prayer and Spirit-led application. He wants us to be aware of just how worthless religious activity can be when it is not prompted by prayerful understanding of God's revelation. And He wants us to be mindful of how quickly prayer can degenerate into earthbound, man-centered complaints and demands when torn away from a practical grasp of biblical truth.

We can't read his letters for long without getting the picture. Spiritual strength comes and grows when we effectively combine those essential activities. However, recognizing the *need* to combine them in the right proportions is always much easier than is actually *doing* so. If we are to successfully defend against this devious assault of neglect, we need a plan.

Step 1: How Are We Doing Right Now?

The first logical step in our plan is to evaluate how we're doing right now. One good way to analyze your current condition is to keep a written record for a couple of weeks. Get a small notebook and write the date at the top of the page. Then list the essential elements of your spiritual workout routine down the left margin: (1) Taking in Scripture, (2) Putting what you have learned into practice, and (3) Resting in prayer. Next to each element record the actual amount of time you spend that day engaged in that element, along with descriptive examples of *how* you spend that time. Do this every day for at least two weeks.

Then take some time to analyze your collected data to see if your workout routine is well-proportioned and whether you are neglecting any of those essential activities. But be careful, because a well-proportioned workout routine is not necessarily one in which you spend the *same number* of clock hours engaged in each element.

You know, of course, that no one gets physically fit by spending just as much time eating good food as walking the dog or riding a bike—nor by working out in the gym for the same length of time as sleeping each night. Generally speaking, it takes *less time* to eat well and *more time* to rest well than it does to exercise well.

When you develop a well-proportioned physical workout routine, you consider how much time *you* need to devote to each element of it. To do that, you look at a number of factors. Things like your age, your overall health, your gender, your size, and your occupation all influence how much of each element should go into *your* workout routine. The right physical fitness routine *for you* won't look just like your husband's, or your best friend's, or your daughter's. Neither will the right spiritual workout routine *for you* look just like someone else's.

That's why I can't give you a one-size-fits-all, perfectly proportioned spiritual workout routine that you can start using immediately just by adding your own personal effort. I could tell you about the routine I use, but chances are it won't fit you as well as it does me. That's because you and I may be at different stages of maturity in Christ, our spiritual health may not be the same, and God has not gifted us identically; nor has He called us to the same kinds of ministry. Each of God's children needs a *custom-tailored* workout routine. That is one of the reasons our loving Father gave each of us a Personal Spiritual Trainer, His indwelling Spirit.

The Holy Spirit knows the mind of God perfectly, and so He knows God's intents and purposes for you and for me (1 Corinthians 2:10–12). He also searches *our* hearts and knows us better than we know ourselves (Romans 8:27; Psalm 139:23–24). Therefore, He knows how to help us develop a personalized workout routine that will uniquely equip us to serve God effectively. Wise Christians don't try to borrow someone else's workout routine. Rather, they lean on God's Spirit to help them "work out" their own.

Step 2: Identifying Needed Corrections

Developing your own personal workout routine involves identifying corrections you need to make to get from where you are right now to where God's Holy Spirit wants you to be. Identifying those needed corrections can be more difficult than actually making them—not because it requires so much time and effort, but because it demands that we ask ourselves hard questions and be willing to answer them honestly. Honest answers require submission to the Spirit's conviction in areas that may make us very uncomfortable.

Now before those butterflies in your stomach convince you to skip the rest of this lesson, remember that we can't pursue God's kingdom effectively with a focus on our own personal comfort. So let's take a look at some of the questions you need to ask yourself—in spite of your nervous stomach.

First of all, are you taking in too little Scripture to support the work God has called you to do? In other words, are you trying to exercise with too little nourishment? You should answer yes to that question if you *characteristically* lack confidence in ministry . . . if you can't answer questions people ask you . . . if you can't support what you're saying and doing with specific scriptural references . . . or if you find yourself constantly plagued by indecision. I believe that most Christians *desperately* need to eat better. Most of us are trying to do the work of the kingdom on a starvation diet, and we're simply too emaciated to be very effective.

How about your exercise? How many bold, radical, disturbing applications have you made this week in the areas of your thinking, your attitudes, and your behavior? If someone you haven't seen or spoken to in two years ran into you at the mall, would they notice any changes in you? Do you worry less now than you did last month? Are you more selective about movies and television? Have your gifts of time and money to others become more sacrificial? When was the last time you went even so far as to give up something you really *wanted* so someone else could have something she really *needed?* Answering those questions honestly with the Spirit's assistance will tell you a lot about how well you are practicing what you're learning from God's Word.

Now, think for a moment about your prayer life. How, when, where, and why do you pray? Do you have a time set apart for deep concentration on prayer? Do you pray constantly all through the day? Do you fall asleep praying at night—and wake up in the morning praying where you left off? What is the subject matter of most of your prayers? Do you seek *first* God's kingdom and His righteousness in your prayers, and *then* seek from Him the resources you need to do the work He has called you to do? Do you pray specifically enough to recognize your Father's answers when He gives them to you? Is the greater display of God's glory the driving motivation behind your prayers? Honest answers to these kinds of questions will tell you a lot about your devotion to prayer.

If you will seek the Spirit's help as you work through this exercise, rest assured He *will* help you identify several specific corrections you need to make in your spiritual workout routine. And don't be surprised if those corrections seem to cluster in one or two areas. Most of us are weaker in one or two of those areas than we are in the others. And most of us hate to admit it. We would rather reach for an excuse than for a solution. But doing what we'd rather do won't build up our spiritual strength. It will only increase our weakness. Spiritual strength comes and grows when we swallow our pride and humbly use what we learn from our Personal Spiritual Trainer to implement changes in our workout routine.

Step 3: Implementation

The best way to begin implementing those changes is to devise a specific step-by-step plan of action. That plan begins to take shape when you ask yourself a few more hard questions: *What specific actions* must you take to get from where you are now to where God wants you to be? *When* and *where* will you take those actions? *How* (in terms of your attitude) will you take action? *Who* will be involved in those actions with you? *What* will be their role?

As you answer these questions and start formulating your plan, be alert to the danger of overcorrecting. If you need to add more Bible study to your routine and plan to sign up for a different study each night of the week, you'll soon have no time to do anything else. And of course, you should also plan to enlist the help of a mature Christian friend, a mentor, or a relative who knows you well and loves you enough to encourage you in your efforts and to hold you accountable for following through on your plans.

Step 4: Dealing with Failure

The final step in your plan should be to memorize 1 John 1:9—because you're going to need it! That verse says, "If we confess our sins, He is faithful and righteous to forgive us our sins and to cleanse us from all unrighteousness." As you work at developing and maintaining a well-proportioned spiritual workout routine, you can be sure that you will fail again and again. You can also be sure that the Devil will use those failures to tempt you to give up in frustration.

But you can foil his assaults by reminding yourself of God's gracious promise to forgive you and restore you to service when you confess your sins to Him. Remember that greater is He who is in you than he who is in the world, and that God will accomplish all His good pleasure—including the good work He has begun in you (1 John 4:4; Isaiah 46:9–10; Philippians 1:6).

Once again, as we've emphasized so often throughout these lessons, successfully thwarting the author of all devious strength stealers requires us to set our minds on the things above rather than the things on the earth.

Exercises

Review

1. Describe two ways in which neglect saps spiritual strength. Which of these two is most difficult for you to defend against?

2. Explain in your own words how the interaction between diet, exercise, and rest contributes to building and maintaining strength. Use the analogy between physical and spiritual strength to clarify your explanation.

3. What do we learn from Paul in Colossians 3–4 about the importance of combining a consistent, well-balanced diet of Scripture, strenuous obedience to God, and rest-

ing in prayer? What kinds of things should individual Christians consider when trying to combine these three things?

4. Describe a procedure you could use to analyze how well your spiritual workout routine is integrated at this point in your life.

5. Explain the importance of including in your plan for change a step that concerns dealing with failure.

Application
Unlike most "application" exercises in the Light for Your Path Series, exercises 1–4 are closely related. If at all possible, you should work on all of them. If you cannot work on all of them, read exercises 1–3 carefully, and work on the one that deals with the area in which you are currently weakest.

1. Answer the following questions honestly, giving one or two personal examples to support each of your answers.

   a. Do you *characteristically* lack confidence in ministry? (Not just occasionally, but *characteristically*.)
   b. Are you *routinely* unable to answer questions people ask you about your faith and about Christianity?
   c. Are you *typically* unable to support your opinions and your behavior with specific scriptural references?
   d. Are you *constantly* plagued by indecision in your walk with the Lord?
   e. What do your answers to these questions tell you about the adequacy of your diet of Scripture?

2. Answer the following questions honestly, giving one or two personal examples to support each of your answers.

a. How many bold, radical, disturbing applications have you made this week (or even this month) in the areas of your thinking, your attitudes, and your behavior?
b. If someone you haven't seen or spoken to in two years ran into you at the mall, would he or she notice any changes in you? If so, describe those noticeable changes.
c. Do you worry less now than you did last month?
d. Are you more selective about movies and television this year than you were last year?
e. Have your gifts of time and money to others become more sacrificial? If you answered yes, when was the last time you gave up something you really *wanted* so that someone else could have something she really *needed?* When was the last time you gave up something you *needed* to meet the need of someone else?
f. What do your answers to these questions tell you about how well you are applying what you are learning from Scripture?

3. Answer the following questions honestly, giving one or two personal examples to support each of your answers.

a. How, when, where, and why do you pray?
b. Do you have a time set apart for deep concentration on prayer?
c. Do you pray constantly all through the day?
d. Do you fall asleep praying at night—and wake up in the morning praying where you left off?
e. What is the subject matter of most of your prayers?
f. Do you seek *first* God's kingdom and His righteousness in your prayers, and *then* seek from Him

the resources you need to do the work He has called you to do?

g. Do you pray specifically enough to recognize your Father's answers when He gives them to you?

h. Is the greater display of God's glory the driving motivation behind your prayers?

i. What do the answers to these questions tell you about your devotion to prayer?

4. Consider carefully your answers to the questions in exercises 1–3. In light of your answers, do you believe your spiritual workout routine is well proportioned? Do you believe you are neglecting one or more of the essential elements of a good spiritual workout routine? If you answered yes, devise a plan that will help you make needed corrections.

5. Review your memory verses from previous lessons. Then begin memorizing one or more of the following:

> Psalm 139:23–24
> 1 John 1:9
> 1 John 4:4

Digging Deeper

1. Read carefully the words of the Puritan teacher John Brown that opened this lesson. Then answer these questions: How might succumbing to the assaults of the strength stealer of neglect darken our views or shake our confidence with respect to the great principles of our Christian faith? How might this lead to cutting the sinews of dutiful exertion, making it difficult or impossible for us to run the race set before us?

13
Disease and Injury

God uses suffering to purge sin from our lives, strengthen our commitment to him, force us to depend on grace, bind us together with other believers, produce discernment, foster sensitivity, discipline our minds, spend our time wisely, stretch our hope, cause us to know Christ better, make us long for truth, lead to repentance of sin, teach us to give thanks in time of sorrow, increase faith, and strengthen character. It is a beautiful image.
—Joni Eareckson Tada

It's been almost a year since my friend Mike fell more than ten feet from a ladder onto the concrete driveway in front of his home. He suffered a broken wrist, a large gash in the back of his head, and serious damage to his spine. Mike spent months recovering from that fall and in the process amazed his doctors. Although they were all sure that repairing his damaged back would require surgical intervention, Mike cheerfully opted instead to pursue prayer and a rugged regimen of physical therapy.

His choice did not surprise those who know him well. Mike is a strong man, both physically and spiritually. His rigorously disciplined lifestyle has kept him in excellent physical and spiritual shape. For many years, he has been consistently faithful in working out both body and soul, and consequently was well equipped to face and overcome the physical and emotional trauma of sudden, serious injury.

Mike's excellent physical condition and overall good health contributed significantly to his nonsurgical physical recovery. If he had not been eating right, exercising strenuously, and resting well for most of his fifty-plus years, he would not have responded so well or so quickly to physical therapy. His "amazing" recovery bears eloquent testimony to the great worth of maintaining physical fitness.

But what speaks even more eloquently is his God-focused endurance of this difficult trial. Mike spent many months battling physical pain, frustrating inactivity, distressing dependency, and fearful uncertainties—without giving in to despair and depression. His eyes remained firmly fixed on the things above instead of the things on the earth.

Mike's spiritual strength (and also that of Patti, his wife) reflected God's glory well as they concentrated on discerning and submitting to His purposes for their ordeal. If they had not been well nourished by Scripture, accustomed to faithful obedience, and devoted to prayer, they would not have responded so well, nor so quickly, to God's "spiritual therapy."

Assaults on More Than One Front

The primary difference between the first two strength stealers we have discussed (laziness and neglect) and the two we're about to discuss (disease and injury) is their source. Laziness and neglect are assaults of our own fallen flesh that are encouraged and applauded by the world and the Devil. Disease and injury, on the other hand, attack from outside ourselves and are then intensified when our flesh uses them as excuses for self-pity or an improper focus.

Thus, although the sources of these assaults differ, the world, the flesh, and the Devil cooperate heartily in their devious desire to derail and distract us from kingdom service. Mike's tragic fall clearly was not the result of his own laziness or neglect, but its affects would have been amplified if he had caved in to the natural desires of his own fallen flesh. Feeling sorry for himself and ignoring God's revealed truth about suffering would have worsened both his physical and his spiritual condition.

We have seen that our flesh is naturally lazy and inclined to neglect strenuous strength-building disciplines. And you may know from personal experience that those fleshly dispositions intensify when we are sick or injured—particularly when illness or trauma not only weakens us temporarily, but has far-reaching affects. If Mike had been paralyzed by his fall or had lost one of his limbs, rebuilding his strength would have been much more of a challenge.

We should keep in mind, however, that challenges well met do not steal strength from us, but build it. We all know people who are quite physically fit, although their bodies have been scarred and damaged by injury or disease. In fact, some of them put to shame those of us who are whole! We look at them and realize that they are stronger than we are. They have not simply "bounced back" from adversity; they are actually stronger because of it.

It should come as no surprise to us, therefore, that God works similarly in the spiritual realm. He is, after all, our all-powerful, loving Father, who sovereignly works all things together for our good and His glory. When we faithfully work out with the strength-building equipment that

God gives all His children, we prepare ourselves to face the assaults of spiritual disease and injury with our minds set on Him and His sovereign purposes. And as we persevere in working out with our spiritual resources in the midst of very challenging difficulties, we will see those strength stealers transformed into strength builders.

A Sure Defense

When we speak of "spiritual disease and injury," we are gathering a great many strength stealers into one very large category. The term encompasses "diseases" like false teaching, bad doctrine, and worldly perspectives, as well the "injuries" associated with the physical, mental, and emotional traumas God's children experience in this fallen world.

Paul mentioned several of these strength stealers specifically when he warned the Colossians against allowing anyone to take them "captive through philosophy and empty deception, according to the tradition of men, according to the elementary principles of the world, rather than according to Christ" (2:8); when he exhorted them to put aside immorality, impurity, passion, evil desire, greed, anger, wrath, malice, slander, abusive speech, and lying (3:5–9); and when he alluded to the inevitable physical persecution God's children endure in the service of Christ (1:24).

Naturally, we cannot look at each of these strength stealers specifically in this short lesson.[1] But we can and will look at them as a category of attackers whose affects are quite similar, and to whom our basic attitude and general response should be identical.

All spiritual disease and injury tend to divert our focus from the things above to the things of the earth and thereby to distract us from faithful service to God. Defending ourselves against these varied assaults is not complicated, though it is difficult to do. All it takes to maintain a sure defense against them is a *practical biblical understanding* of God's absolute sovereignty and of His great love for His children.

Paul summarized this good practical understanding in the eighth chapter of Romans with the following words:

> We know that God causes *all things* to work together for good to those who love God, to those who are called according to His purpose. . . .
>
> What then shall we say to these things? If God is for us, who is against us? He who did not spare His own Son, but delivered Him up for us all, how will He not also with Him freely give us all things? . . .
>
> Who shall separate us from the love of Christ? Shall tribulation, or distress, or persecution, or famine, or nakedness, or peril, or sword? Just as it is written,
>
>> "For Thy sake we are being put to death all day long;
>> We were considered as sheep to be slaughtered."
>
> But in all these things we overwhelmingly conquer through Him who loved us. For I am convinced that neither death, nor life, nor angels, nor principalities, nor things present, nor things to come, nor powers, nor height, nor depth, nor any other created thing, shall be able to separate us from the love of God, which is in Christ Jesus our Lord. (vv. 28, 31, 35–39)

Do you see God's sovereignty shining through those verses? Do you see His great love for His children? Paul says that God *causes* all things to work together for good for those He has called out of the world to accomplish His purposes. Paul also says that nothing (that's *no* thing, not a single created being or thing anywhere in the universe, not even you yourself) can separate us from His love. Paul said those amazing things under the inspiration of God's Holy Spirit for the purpose of our edification. His words recorded in Romans 8 are absolute truth from the mouth of God.

Understanding his words, believing them, and applying them in practical situations of life is our sure defense against *every* devious assault of spiritual disease and injury.

Now the Hard Part

There. That wasn't so hard to explain, was it? We understand what Paul said. His language in this passage of Romans is not vague or difficult. We could put what he's said into our own words and explain it to a friend or a relative or a child. That part wasn't hard. But the next part is. Do we believe him? It's easy to say we believe when we are sitting in comfortable chairs in comfortable rooms and the events of our lives are going quite well. But what about when our comfort sharply twists into pain and the events of our lives take a bizarre turn for the worse?

What about when it's your home that's destroyed by a fire, earthquake, or flood? What about when it's your church that's splitting over seemingly irreconcilable doctrinal differences? What about when it's your son, who's grown up in the covenant community, who marries a Mormon? What about when it's your husband who loses his job, or contracts a disease that prevents him from working, or suffers a heart attack and dies at age thirty-five?

What about when it's your fourteen-year-old daughter who tells you she's pregnant—or when it's you who finds drugs hidden under your twelve year old's mattress? What about when it's your doctor who tells you it's cancer? What about when it's the airplane carrying your mother and father that crashes with no survivors? What about when it's your son or daughter who is shot and killed in the high school library or a church youth group meeting?

At times like these, spiritual strength comes and grows when we *believe,* that is when we know and rely upon, the absolute truth of God's words. We will honor our Father by displaying the strength He has perfected in our weakness when we trust Him enough to put into practice what He has taught us.

Joni Eareckson Tada summed it up well when she said,

> We amble on along our philosophical path, and then—Bam!—get hit with suffering. No longer is our fundamental view of life providing a sense of meaning or a sense of security in our world. Suffering has not only rocked the boat, it's capsized it. We need assurance that the world is not splitting apart at the seams. We need to know we aren't going to fizzle into a zillion atomic particles and go spinning off into space. We need to be reassured that the world, the universe, is not a nightmarish chaos, but orderly and stable. God must be at the center of things. He must be at the center of our suffering.[2]

What You See Depends on Where You Are Looking

If your eyes are fixed on the things above, you *will* see God at the center of your suffering. You will know that He has sovereignly ordained whatsoever has come to pass in your life, and that He loves you with perfect love. If your mind is set on the things above and you earnestly seek to honor God in your thoughts, attitudes, and behavior, then spiritual disease and injury will not steal the strength from you that God has perfected in you.

That's because you *believe* (know and rely on) the fact that God is both able and willing to accomplish all His good pleasure, including the good work He has begun in you through His sovereign, loving ordaining of every circumstance of your life. You *believe* His promise not to tempt (or try) you more than you are able to bear, but with the temptation (or trial) to provide the way of escape also, so that you may be able to endure it for the greater display of His glory and the enhancement of your joy in His service.[3]

But what if you can't honestly say you believe in God's sovereign ability and perfect love when those kinds of things happen? Does that mean you're not saved? Possibly. But not necessarily. You can test yourself to see if you are in the faith by examining yourself to see if you recognize Jesus Christ living in you (see 2 Corinthians 13:5). Have you acknowledged your helpless sinfulness and thrown yourself on God's gracious provision of forgiveness and restoration through the work of His Son? Have you seen evidence in your life of the transformation that results from union with Christ? Has your hard heart of stone become a responsive heart of flesh that longs to obey God's commands to show forth His glory? If you can answer "yes" to those questions, chances are very good you are saved.

So, if you're sure of your salvation, but you still can't say you believe in God's sovereign ability and loving care in all situations, what's wrong with you? Simply put, you are weak. But there's a solution for weakness. And by now you should know what it is: "If then you have been raised up with Christ [and if you are saved, you have been], keep seeking the things above, where Christ is, seated at the right hand of God. Set your mind on the things above, not on the things that are on earth."

You have the raw materials you need to be strong: You

have spiritual life, the good bones of knowledge, the muscles of faith, the blood of love, and the skin of fellowship. With those raw materials, you can be strong in defending yourself and others against assaults from the world, the flesh, and the Devil *if* you put those components to work in an effective spiritual workout routine.

No one has summarized spiritual strength building better than our brother Paul. Listen to what he told the Ephesians:

Finally, be strong in the Lord, and in the strength of His might. Put on the full armor of God, that you may be able to stand firm against the schemes of the devil. For our struggle is not against flesh and blood, but against the rulers, against the powers, against the world forces of this darkness, against the spiritual forces of wickedness in the heavenly places. Therefore, take up the full armor of God, that you may be able to resist in the evil day, and having done everything, to stand firm. Stand firm therefore, having girded your loins with truth, and having put on the breastplate of righteousness, and having shod your feet with the preparation of the gospel of peace; in addition to all, taking up the shield of faith with which you will be able to extinguish all the flaming missiles of the evil one. And take the helmet of salvation, and the sword of the Spirit, which is the word of God. With all prayer and petition pray at all times in the Spirit, and with this in view, be on the alert with all perseverance and petition for all the saints, and pray on my behalf, that utterance may be given to me in the opening of my mouth, to make known with boldness the mystery of the gospel, for which I am an ambassador in chains; that in proclaiming it I may speak boldly, as I ought to speak (6:10–20).

As we come to the end of our study of spiritual strength, meditate on Paul's words before you work on the exercises. Think about how his few words encapsulate everything we have learned in these many pages. Then thank God for His Word and its blessed ability to strengthen you for His service in the power of His Holy Spirit. Confess your sins of laziness, neglect, and failure to defend against spiritual disease and injury. Acknowledge His power in perfecting strength in your weakness, and ask Him to use you to accomplish His purposes.

Remember that spiritual strength is primarily a matter of focus. It comes and grows as you "keep seeking the things above, where Christ is, seated at the right hand of God." Your Father has promised that you can and will be strong in the Lord and in the strength of His might when you "set your mind on the things above, not on the things that are on earth." Praise Him for His sure provision of your every need in His service.

Then get up and get moving!

Notes

1. For an in-depth analysis of how to face suffering in a way that honors God and increases your joy, see my book *James on Trials: How Faith Matures in the Storms of Life* (Los Alamos, N.M.: Deo Volente, 1998). Another helpful compassionate book on the "theology of suffering" is Joni Eareckson Tada and Steve Estes, *When God Weeps: Why Our Sufferings Matter to the Almighty* (Grand Rapids: Zondervan, 1997).

2. Joni Eareckson Tada and Steve Estes, *When God Weeps,* 125.

3. The Greek word translated "temptation" in 1 Corinthians 10:13 (*peirasmos*) is a neutral word in Greek that describes a trial (a difficult circumstance) that can become either a temptation to sin or an opportunity to trust God depending upon our response to it.

Exercises

Review

1. Describe in your own words the importance of maintaining physical and spiritual fitness as it relates to facing and overcoming sudden, serious disease or injury.

2. What is the primary difference between the assaults of laziness and neglect and the assaults of disease and injury? How do the world, the flesh, and the Devil eagerly cooperate in all of these assaults?

3. What has to happen before we will see the strength stealer of disease and injury transformed into a strength builder?

4. What should our basic attitude and general response be to all kinds of spiritual disease and injury? (See Romans 8:31–39.)

5. Describe the difference between *understanding* Paul's words in Romans 8:31–39 and *believing* them. Why is one more difficult than the other?

6. Study Romans 8:31–39; 2 Corinthians 13:5; and Ephesians 6:10–20. Drawing on the truths contained in these verses, explain how we have been equipped by God to glorify Him in difficult circumstances.

Application

1. Do you believe what Paul said in Romans 8 about God's sovereign control of the circumstances of your life and His perfect love for you? Read through the questions on pages 174–75. Do any of them hit home with you? If so, which ones? If not, is there a difficult circumstance in your life right now that makes believing the truth of Paul's words hard for you? Describe your difficult situation. Then reread Romans 8:31–39 in light of this situation. Explain how these verses apply to the difficulties you are experiencing. How might your circumstances be seen as a spiritual disease or injury that could steal the strength God has perfected in your weakness? What actions must you take to prevent this from happening? Make a specific plan of defense against this assault of the world, the flesh, and the Devil. How will implementing this plan transform this strength stealer into a strength builder?

2. Study Paul's summary of spiritual strength building in Ephesians 6:10–20 in light of what we have learned in this study. See if you can identify his references to the components of strength, the essential elements of a good spiritual workout routine, and ways we defend against devious strength stealers. Will his summary help you apply what you have learned in this study? If so, how? Explain how this passage enhances your *practical* understanding of spiritual strength, and how it will help you implement strength-building change in your life.

3. Review all your memory verses. Then make a schedule for reviewing them in the future, and enlist a partner to hold you accountable.

Digging Deeper

1. Drawing on what you have learned in this study, write a few concise paragraphs supporting the assertion that spiritual strength is primarily a matter of focus. Then consider several ways you might use what you have learned to strengthen the body of Christ.

APPENDIX A

What Must I Do to Be Saved?

A strange sound drifted through the Philippian jail as midnight approached. The sound of human voices—but not the expected groans of the two men who had earlier been beaten with rods and fastened in stocks. Rather, the peaceful singing of praises to their God.

While the other prisoners quietly listened to them, the jailer dozed off, content with the bizarre calm generated by these two preachers, who, hours before, had stirred so much commotion in the city.

Suddenly a deafening roar filled the prison as the ground began to shake violently. Sturdy doors convulsed and popped open. Chains snapped and fell at prisoners' feet. Startled into full wakefulness, the jailer stared, horrified, at the wide-open doors that guaranteed his prisoners' escape—and his own death. Under Roman law, jailers paid with their lives when prisoners escaped. Resolutely, he drew his sword, thinking it better to die by his own hand than by Roman execution.

"Stop! Don't harm yourself—we are all here!" a voice boomed from the darkened inner cell. The jailer called for lights and was astonished to discover his prisoners standing quietly amid their broken chains. Trembling with fear, he rushed in and fell at the feet of the two preachers. As soon as he was able, he led them out of the ruined prison and asked in utter astonishment, "Sirs, what must I do to be saved?"

— — —

In the entire history of the world, no one has ever asked a more important question. The jailer's words that day may well have been motivated by his critical physical need, but the response of Paul and Silas addressed his even more critical spiritual need: "Believe in the Lord Jesus, and you shall be saved, you and your household" (Acts 16:13).[1]

If you have never "believed in the Lord Jesus," your spiritual need, just like the jailer's, is critical. As long as your life is stained with sin, God cannot receive you into His presence. The Bible says that sin has placed a separation between you and God (Isaiah 59:2). It goes on to say that your nature has been so permeated by sin that you no longer have any desire to serve and obey God (Romans 3:10–12); therefore, you are not likely to recognize or care that a separation exists. Your situation is truly desperate because those who are separated from God will spend eternity in hell.

Since your sinful nature is unresponsive to God, the only way you can be saved from your desperate situation is for God to take the initiative. And this He has done! Even though all men and women deserve the punishment of hell because of their sin, God's love has prompted Him to save some who will serve Him in obedience. He did this by sending His Son, the Lord Jesus Christ, to remove the barrier of sin between God and His chosen ones (Colossians 2:13–14).

What is there about Jesus that enables Him to do this? First of all, He is God. While He was on earth He said, "He who has seen Me has seen the Father" (John 14:9), and "I and the Father are one" (John 10:30). Because He said these things, you must conclude one of three things about His true identity: (1) He was a lunatic who believed He was God when He really wasn't; (2) He was a liar who was willing to die a hideous death for what He knew was a lie; or (3) His words are true and He is God.

Lunatics don't live the way Jesus did, and liars don't die the way He did, so if the Bible's account of Jesus' life and words is true, you can be sure He *is* God.

Since Jesus is God, He is perfectly righteous and holy. God's perfect righteousness and holiness demand that sin be punished (Ezekiel 18:4), and Jesus' perfect righteousness and holiness qualified Him to bear the punishment for the sins of those who will be saved (Romans 6:23). Jesus is the only person who never committed a sin; therefore, the punishment He bore when He died on the cross could be accepted by God as satisfaction of His justice in regard to the sins of others.

If someone you love commits a crime and is sentenced to die, you may offer to die in his place. However, if you have also committed crimes worthy of death, your death cannot satisfy the law's demands for your crimes *and* your loved one's. You can only die in his place if you are innocent of any wrongdoing.

Since Jesus lived a perfect life, God's justice could be satisfied by allowing Him to die for the sins of those who will be saved. Because God is perfectly righteous and holy, He could not act in love at the expense of justice. By sending Jesus to die, God demonstrated His love *by acting to satisfy His own justice* (Romans 3:26).

Jesus did more than die, however. He also rose from the dead. By raising Jesus from the dead, God declared that He had accepted Jesus' death in the place of those who will be saved. Because Jesus lives eternally with God, those for whom Jesus died can be assured they will also spend eternity in heaven (John 14:1–3). The separation of sin has been removed!

Ah, but the all-important question remains unanswered: What must *you do* to be saved? If God has sent His Son into the world for sinners, and Jesus Christ died in their place, what is left for you to do? You must respond in faith to what God has done. This is what Paul meant when he told the jailer, "Believe in the Lord Jesus, and you shall be saved."

Believing in the Lord Jesus demands three responses from you: (1) an understanding of the facts regarding your hopeless sinful condition and God's action to remove the sin barrier that separates you from Him; (2) acceptance of those facts as true and applicable to you; and (3) a willingness to trust and depend upon God to save you from sin. This involves willingly placing yourself under His authority and acknowledging His sovereign right to rule over you.

But, you say, how can I do this if sin has eliminated my ability to know and appreciate God's work on my behalf? Rest assured that if you desire to have the sin barrier that separates you from God removed, He is already working to change your natural inability to respond. He is extending His gracious offer of salvation to you and will give you the faith to receive it.

If you believe God is working to call you to Himself, read the words He has written to you in the Bible (begin with the book of John in the New Testament) and pray that His Holy Spirit will help you understand what is written there. Continue to read and pray until you are ready to *repent,* that is, to turn away from sin and commit yourself to serving God.

Is there any other way you can be saved? God Himself says no, there is not. The Bible He wrote says that Jesus is the only way the sin barrier between you and God can be removed (John 14:6; Acts 4:12). He is your hope, and He is your *only* hope.

If you have questions or need any help in this matter, please write to The Evangelism Team, Providence Presbyterian Church, P. O. Box 14651, Albuquerque, NM 87191, before the day is over. God has said in His Bible that a day of judgment is coming, and after that day no one will be saved (Acts 17:30–31; 2 Thessalonians 1:7–9). The time to act is now.

Notes

1. For a full biblical account of this event, see Acts 16:11–40.

What Is the Reformed Faith?

"The Reformed faith"[1] can be defined as a theology that describes and explains the sovereign God's revelation of His actions in history to glorify Himself by redeeming selected men and women from the just consequences of their self-inflicted depravity.

It is first and foremost *theology* (the study of God), not *anthropology* (the study of man). Reformed thinking concentrates on developing a true knowledge of God that serves as the necessary context for all other knowledge. It affirms that the created world, including humanity itself, cannot be accurately understood apart from its relationship with the Creator.

The Reformed faith describes and explains God's revelation of Himself and His actions to humanity; it does not consist of people's attempts to define God as they wish. The Reformed faith asserts that God has revealed Himself in two distinct ways. He reveals His existence, wisdom, and power through the created universe—a process known as *natural revelation* (Romans 1:18–32); and He reveals His requirements and plans for mankind through His written Word, the Bible—a process known as *special revelation* (2 Timothy 3:16–17).

Reformed theologians uphold the Bible as the inspired, infallible, inerrant, authoritative, and fully sufficient communication of truth from God to us. When they say the Bible is "inspired," they mean that the Bible was actually written by God through the agency of human authorship in a miraculous way that preserved the thoughts of God from the taint of human sinfulness (2 Peter 1:20–21).

When they say the Bible is infallible, they mean it is *incapable* of error, and when they say it is inerrant, they mean the Bible, *in actual fact,* contains no errors. The Bible is authoritative because it comes from God whose authority over His creation is absolute (Isaiah 46:9–10). And it is completely sufficient because it contains everything necessary for us to know and live according to God's requirements (2 Peter 1:3–4).

By studying God's revelation of Himself and His work, Reformed theologians have learned two foundational truths that structure their thinking about God's relationship with human beings: God is absolutely sovereign, and people are totally depraved.[2]

Reformed thought affirms that God, by definition, is *absolutely sovereign*—that is, He controls and superintends every circumstance of life either by direct miraculous intervention or by the ordinary outworking of His providence. Reformed theologians understand that a "god" who is not sovereign cannot be God because his power would not be absolute. Since the Reformed faith accepts the Bible's teaching regarding the sovereignty of God, it denies that *anything* occurs outside of God's control.

The Reformed faith affirms the biblical teaching that Adam was created with the ability to sin and chose to do so by disobeying a clear command of God (Genesis 3:1–7). Choosing to sin changed basic human nature and left us unable not to sin—or *totally depraved.* Total depravity does not mean that all people are as bad as they possibly could be, but that every facet of their character is tainted with sin, leaving them incapable and undesirous of fellowship with

God. The Reformed faith denies that totally depraved men and women have any ability to seek after or submit to God of their own free will. Left to themselves, totally depraved men and women will remain out of fellowship with God for all eternity.

The only way for any of these men and women to have their fellowship with God restored is for God Himself to take the initiative. And the Bible declares that He has graciously chosen to do so (John 14:16). *For His own glory,* He has chosen some of those depraved men and women to live in fellowship with Him. His choice is determined by His own good pleasure and not by any virtue in the ones He has chosen. For this reason, *grace* is defined in Reformed thought as "unmerited favor."

God accomplished the salvation of His chosen ones by sending His Son, the Lord Jesus Christ, to bear God's righteous wrath against sin so that He could forgive those He had chosen. Even though Christ's work was perfect and complete, its intended effectiveness is limited to those who are chosen by God for salvation. Christ would not have been required to suffer any more or any less had a different number been chosen for redemption, but the benefit of His suffering is applied only to those who are called by God to believe in Him.

All of those who are thus effectually called by God will eventually believe and be saved, even though they may resist for a time (John 6:37). They cannot forfeit the salvation they have received (John 10:27–30; Romans 8:31–39).

Reformed thought affirms the clear teaching of the Bible that salvation is by faith alone through Christ alone (John 14:6; Acts 4:12; Ephesians 2:8–9), and that human works play no part in salvation although they are generated by it (Ephesians 2:10). Salvation transforms a person's nature, giving him or her the ability and the desire to serve and obey God. The unresponsive heart of stone is changed into a sensitive heart of flesh that responds readily to God's voice (Ezekiel 36:25–27) and desires to glorify Him out of gratitude for the indescribable gift of salvation.

Reformed thought affirms that *God works in history to redeem* His chosen ones through a series of covenants. These covenants define His law, assess penalties for breaking His law, and provide for the imputation of Jesus' vicarious fulfillment of God's requirements to those God intends to redeem.[3]

The Reformed faith affirms that we were created and exist solely to glorify God, and denies that God exists to serve us. It affirms that God acts to glorify Himself by putting His attributes on display, and that His self-glorifying actions are thoroughly righteous since He is the only Being in creation worthy of glorification. It denies that God is *primarily* motivated to act by man's needs, but affirms that all of God's actions are motivated *primarily* for His own glory.

The Reformed faith emerged as a distinct belief system during the sixteenth and seventeenth centuries when men like Luther, Calvin, Zwingli, and Knox fought against the Roman Catholic Church to restore Christian doctrine to biblical truth. These men were labeled "Reformers," but they would have been better labeled "Restorers." Their goal was to correct abuses and distortions of Christianity that were rampant in the established Roman church and to restore the purity of the gospel and church life taught by the apostles in the New Testament. Reformed thinkers since their day have sought to align their understanding of God and His actions in history as closely as possible to His truth revealed in the Bible.

Notes

1. This brief overview of basic Reformed beliefs is not intended to be a full explanation of or apologetic for the Reformed faith. For a more detailed description and analysis of the Reformed faith, see R. C. Sproul, *Grace Unknown* (Grand Rapids: Baker, 1997); Loraine Boettner, *The Reformed Faith* (Phillipsburg, N.J.: Presbyterian and Reformed, 1983); *Back to Basics: Rediscovering the Richness of the Reformed Faith,* ed. David G. Hagopian (Phillipsburg, N.J.: P&R Publishing, 1996); *The Westminster Confession of Faith* (with its accompanying catechisms); or the theological writings of John Calvin, B. B. Warfield, Charles Hodge, and Louis Berkhof.

2. Both of these truths are taught throughout the pages of Scripture; however, the sovereignty of God can be seen very clearly in Isaiah 40–60 and in Job 38–42, while the total depravity of man is described quite graphically in Romans 3:10–18.

3. An excellent discussion of these covenants is contained in chapter 5 of R. C. Sproul, *Grace Unknown.*

Recommended Reading

Bridges, Jerry. *Trusting God*. Colorado Springs: NavPress, 1988.

Burroughs, Jeremiah. *The Rare Jewel of Christian Contentment*. 1648. Reprint. Carlisle, Pa.: Banner of Truth, 1964.

Colson, Charles, and Nancy Pearcey. *How Now Shall We Live?* Wheaton, Ill.: Tyndale House, 1999.

Guinness, Os. *The Call: Finding and Fulfilling the Central Purpose of Your Life*. Nashville: Word, 1998.

Hoekema, Anthony A. *Saved by Grace*. Grand Rapids: Eerdmans, 1989.

Kistler, Don, ed. *Onward Christian Soldiers: Protestants Affirm the Church*. Morgan, Pa.: Soli Deo Gloria, 1999.

MacArthur, John, Jr., *The Love of God*. Dallas: Word, 1996.

————. *The Pillars of Christian Character*. Wheaton, Ill.: Crossway, 1998.

Murray, John. *Redemption Accomplished and Applied*. Grand Rapids: Eerdmans, 1955.

Packer, J. I. *Knowing God*. Downers Grove, Ill.: InterVarsity Press, 1973.

————. *Rediscovering Holiness*. Ann Arbor, Mich.: Servant, 1992.

Piper, John. *Desiring God: Meditations of a Christian Hedonist*. 2d ed. Sisters, Ore.: Multnomah, 1996.

Postman, Neil. *Amusing Ourselves to Death: Public Discourse in the Age of Show Business.* New York: Penguin, 1985.

Tada, Joni Eareckson, and Steve Estes, *When God Weeps: Why Our Sufferings Matter to the Almighty.* Grand Rapids: Zondervan, 1997.

Tozer, A. W. *The Knowledge of the Holy.* San Francisco: Harper and Row, 1961.

Wells, David F. *God in the Wasteland: The Reality of Truth in a World of Fading Dreams.* Grand Rapids: Eerdmans, 1994.

——— . *No Place for Truth or Whatever Happened to Evangelical Theology?* Grand Rapids: Eerdmans, 1993.

Whitney, Donald S. *Spiritual Disciplines for the Christian Life.* Colorado Springs: NavPress, 1991.

Winslow, Octavius. *No Condemnation in Christ: As Unfolding in the Eighth Chapter of the Epistle to the Romans.* 1853. Reprint. Carlisle, Pa.: Banner of Truth, 1991.